# WHEN CULTURES MEET
## REMEMBERING SAN GABRIEL DEL YUNGE OWEENGE

*Papers from the October 20, 1984 Conference
held at San Juan Pueblo, New Mexico*

Sunstone Press
Santa Fe, New Mexico

*Sunstone Press thanks Marian Rodee, Curator of Collections, Maxwell Museum of Anthropology, for her assistance.*

First Edition

Printed in the United States of America

---

Library of Congress Cataloging in Publication Data:

When cultures meet.

    1. Tewa Indians--History--Congresses. 2. San Gabriel
del Yunque (N.M.)--Congresses. 3. San Juan Pueblo (N.M.)
--History--Congresses. 4. Spaniards--New Mexico--
San Gabriel del Yunque--Congresses. 5. Indians of
North America--New Mexico--History--Congresses.

| | | | |
|---|---|---|---|
| E99.T35W46 | 1986 | 978.9'00497 | 86-14466 |

ISBN: 0-86534-091-9

---

The San Gabriel History Project is made possible by a grant from the New Mexico
Humanities Council, an affiliate of the National Endowment for the Humanities.

Published in 1987 by SUNSTONE PRESS
           Post Office Box 2321
           Santa Fe, NM 87504-2321 / USA

# CONTENTS

# FOREWORD

How should one begin the story of San Gabriel del Yunge Oweenge — with a sounding of hard fact, "In 1597 . . ."; or with the invocation of myth, "Once upon a time . . ."?. Which approach, science or myth, is more important for understanding the first capital of New Mexico? It is this character of being poised between fact and fiction which is most striking about San Gabriel and which is essential for understanding these papers.

Being the first European settlement among the Indian Pueblos and the first Spanish-designated capital of the territory which is now New Mexico, San Gabriel's historical identity is well established. With the positive identification of the settlement's location just across the Rio Grande from present day San Juan, San Gabriel gained archaeological renown. Yet to those who have direct ancestral (or at least cultural) ties to that small, short-lived settlement, its significance is of a much different order. The meeting of two races, and the collision of profoundly different world-views is an event which leaves its mark not only in archaeological artifacts and historic events but also in the hearts and minds of a people. In this sense, the meaning of events 400 years ago are, therefore, still very much present for the residents of the Espanola valley, and to a lesser degree all of northern New Mexico. This is the mythic dimension, in which truth has little to do with years passing and everything to do with a people's understanding of themselves.

In recent years San Juan Pueblo has been planning a community museum. In researching San Gabriel, two challenges immediately became clear. First of all, published materials about San Gabriel were entirely scholarly and specialized and none offered a general overview or picture of the settlement and its residents. How did the settlement actually develop? What was the background of the settlers and what kind of life did they find here? What did the native "hosts" actually offer to the newcomers and what did they get in return? The second challenge was to adequately address both the factual and the mythic facets of San Gabriel. The Pueblo had a clear responsibility to address the interest not only of the general student of this early colonial period but also of those who experience daily the heritage of that period.

Out of these considerations the idea of a history conference arose. Yet clearly this could not be your typical history conference. Given the increasing polarization of science and art, prose and

4

poetry, expert and lay, could an amiable forum be created among scientists, scholars, poets and natives? The success of the conference proved that the topic of San Gabriel provided a rare opportunity for this unusual blending. This success can largely be attributed to two factors, both of which force us to expand our understanding of history.

The first factor is simply the paucity of factual data about the settlement. The events and place are obscured just enough by the dust and forgetfulness of years to put everyone on equal footing. There is just enough factual data to fuel the scientific mind, yet not enough to render the subject cut and dried. At the same time, the historic link between the events then and the regional character today is direct enough to inspire the imagination but also to rule out wild or arbitrary speculation. On this subject, the scientists are forced to fill in sizable gaps between known facts with creative speculation, while the poets must discipline their imagination against archival records and local memory.

The title of the conference, "When Cultures Meet: Remembering San Gabriel Del Yunge Oweenge," suggests the second factor bearing upon the success of the conference. The theme of remembrance transcends the boundaries of science and myth and subsumes history within a context of community. Indeed, the feeling at the conference of a shared heritage was as clear and bright as the New Mexico sky on that October day. In the presentations, the luncheon at the Oke Oweenge Crafts Cooperative and performances by folk musician Cipriano Vigil and the San Juan Indian Youth Dances, the feeling of participation in a shared community grew steadily. It is as if this was a gathering to pool together and celebrate a key segment of the region's communal memory. Painful or glorious, shared history eventually creates a community of shared memory.

The actual event of the conference was only the most visible evidence of this community. In truth, it was evident from the project's very conception in the generosity and cooperation extended to the Pueblo in organizing the event. This project was an organizer's dream-come-true, as enthusiasts of San Gabriel and old friends of San Juan came forward with encouragement and offers of help.

We would like first to thank all the participants in the conference who went well beyond their normal responsibilities as presenters and took an active role in the conference's conception and planning. Their willingness to meet together and discuss their respective contributions in advance is what made it possible to bring together diverse perspectives with minimal overlap and produce this well-rounded overall presentation of the subject.

Special thanks also goes to the many residents of San Juan who helped make the conference unfold so smoothly and offered a special touch of hospitality to visitors.

We would like to thank Sunstone Press for providing guidance and production of this publication.

Finally, we would like to thank the New Mexico Humanities Council whose generous support made this project possible. In addition, the entire staff of the Humanities Council have earned our deep appreciation for their guidance, assistance and patience throughout the long course of the project.

We hope you enjoy this volume and the diverse ways revealed to us for leaping over the boundaries of time. We welcome you to explore San Gabriel del Yunge Oweenge, the place, the event and the heritage, through the means of scientific inquiry, scholarly investigation and imaginative speculation.

Herman Agoyo, Tribal Administrator
Lynnwood Brown, Project Coordinator

# SAN GABRIEL REVISITED, 1598-1984
## Orlando Romero

The concept of San Gabriel means different things to different people. To this writer San Gabriel is a mystery with a captial M, for a daily diary or journal of the activities, indeed the very first encounter between the Native people and the first settlers is not revealed to the extent that we would like. We do know from historical records that after a year here these settlers built a church and there was much celebration among both peoples. We know of Onate's administration, his excursions outside of San Gabriel for riches and dreams that were never fulfilled, we know of various historical details except the daily and even mundane goings on of these people.

So what conjectures can we make. We can be assured that both people's way of life affected each other, another simple assumption is that material cultural exchanges must have been made. The settlers brought different seeds, for example, that to this day have affected our contemporary agriculture. And although the colonialists complained of the infertility of the land, we can be assured that seed did mix and that from that different varieties evolved, it could be that is the metaphor of San Gabriel . . . people are like seeds, the wind tosses them about, scatters them to the different corners of the world, and a new variety of fruit is produced, grafted, so to speak, upon the original hardy stock that is part of its origin. In contemporary terms it can be explained by population statistics on this very Pueblo of San Juan today, of 1600 people only 805 are counted as full blooded inhabitants.

Actually the key to understanding San Gabriel is not in statistics but in understanding the cultural legacy that has survived since 1598 to the present. The key world should be amalgamation for I doubt there exists an anthropologist or historian that can deny the fact that intermarriage did indeed occur here. And that in itself no matter where it has occurred has had an impact that has always had a strong influence. Just as Spanish sheep influenced weaving, or the Mexican Plateros influenced silversmithing or as the Matachines became a symbol of duality in shared ritual so too did this first encounter of these people result in a shared union. Poor Onate, little did he realize that as he searched for riches in far-off lands the real riches lay not in the depths of the earth but in the people themselves. Maybe it was for the best that Onate failed . . . the colonialist had to adapt not only to environment but to their new *vecinos*.

Imagine if you can, trade your shoes, and travel back in time, close your eyes for a second and pretend that you're either a Spanish colonial or a native, can you imagine what it must have been like to see each other for the first time? What other Pueblo in this region had aliens living in its midst for over ten years? Putting religious, material and cultural differences aside and knowing human nature, surely, no one can deny that these two people were extremely curious about each other! It seems to me a curious note that the contemporary Chicano must seek his origin in the fabled kingdom of Aztlan when clearly here, in San Gabriel, these two people not only met but produced the new maize seed that was to be the legacy of the future! Can anyone in this prestigious gathering name me two other groups in this country that have shared as much as these two cultures, or for that matter, that have lived so closely in the same region?

Yes, there were disagreements, even abuse to the point that the Pueblo Rebellion was clearly justified. Yet after re-colonization and the reality that the Spanish were here to stay, Pueblo alliances were formed to defeat the much dreaded threat of marauding tribes that were a constant danger to both colonialist and Pueblo Native.

So, these two people lived as *vecinos* for nearly 400 years. And like all neighbors, disagreements were bound to occur, that seems to be a human trait. Yet they coexisted, and coexistence has always been the keystone to peace and understanding. These people got to know each other. It actually went beyond that. How many Hispanics in this area can say that they don't have some relative that is presently married to a Pueblo native? Or how many Pueblo people in all of Northern New Mexico can say that they don't have Hispanic relatives?

Let me expand, strictly on a contemporary, day to day basis; my Grandfather said that as a young man living in Las Trampas, he wore *teguas*, that translates to moccasins. Later when I was ten years old, I used to help my Grandfather in his flour mill in Nambe. Many of the Pueblo people from Santo Domingo to Taos, used to bring my Grandfather their wheat to be ground in his mill. The Pueblo people in those days, about 1957, used to call us *parientes*. That world translates to relatives. There was not one feast day in any Pueblo in this area where my Grandfather and I or our entire family was not welcomed. Many times my Grandfather had business in Espanola and being that he was headed in that direction, he would load up his truck with freshly ground flour, so that as he would put it, "my *parientes* wouldn't have to make an extra trip to the mill."

I remember . . . as if it was yesterday, when my Grandfather used to say "I'm going to visit the Vigils or the Perez, up at the Pueblo." He used to tell me that the Vigils and he had helped each other build their houses.

Maybe it is because I have the poet/writer's background that I remember things so vividly. It could be that I might be accused of romanticizing the bond that these two people shared, but I don't think so, after all I was there. And as such, I have personal knowledge that no anthropologist or historian has had privilege to experience, my memories are deep and true and as relatives there are few secrets that can be kept from each other, especially after 400 years!

In actuality it is our shared legacy, all you have to do is look at our architecture, our food, our deep respect for the land and the water and the entire sacredness of the earth, I don't consider that romantic . . . I consider that a shared reality. Indeed, like *parientes*, relatives, it seems to me we have more in common than things we disagree in or upon. In fact, if there is a lesson to be learned from San Gabriel revisited, it is that this bond must be strengthened, nourished and continued. To do otherwise would be to deny our historical roots and the new maize seed that we cannot deny! It exists! And it also appears to me, that we must bring light to the past, so we learn from it, and with its light grow into the future, after all what are *parientes* for, if not to help each other? Maybe, just maybe, we will hear the world spoken once again, *Pariente!* Relative!

# THE LONG LOST "CITY" OF SAN GABRIEL DEL YUNGUE, SECOND OLDEST EUROPEAN SETTLEMENT IN THE UNITED STATES

*Florence Hawley Ellis*

What do we actually know today of Yungue, that part of San Juan Pueblo in the northern Rio Grande Valley, only five miles north of Espanola, which the Spaniards took over with the intent of making it their first permanent settlement and capital in the late sixteenth century Southwest?

Well, in truth a surprising lot is known about details of this site (LA 59: USGS San Juan Pueblo Quad. T21 N, R8 E, Sec. 15) and its artifacts but by surprisingly few persons. Most of these few are archaeologists.

Twenty-three years ago I was asked to give several lectures in Santa Fe and vicinity on our recently concluded excavations. An exhibit of our own major finds and of the Spanish helmet discovered earlier was displayed in the reception area of the Governors Palace (New Mexico State Museum) in Santa Fe, and following that the Maxwell Museum at the University of New Mexico, where the material since has been housed in their secure storage facilities, put on an exhibit of our collections.

We had not expected to dig up and then re-bury in storage the data and the finds from San Gabriel del Yungue. Some of the state officials at that time were becoming interested in a project for which we were making tentative plans: a free-to-the public museum on the site with arrangements for a sales area where the San Juan people could present their own handicrafts. Our work and finds at San Gabriel had brought Governor Mechem, representatives of the museum, Spain's major newsman, then at the Spanish embassy in Washington, and numerous others out to see the excavations in progress. This show of widespread enthusiasm was capped by an article in *Time Magazine* and articles in numerous papers over the United States. An architect friend contributed an elevation of the small museum proposed for the grounds. We would make some further excavations to complete the outline of the site, and space near the old narrow-gauge Denver and Rio Grande station foundations would be made into a parking lot, the fees from which would provide a sum to go to the Pueblo itself. The little access road serving two occupied houses but chancing to have been set directly over the colony's permanent long lost church of San Miguel could be re-routed without loss of convenience.

But within the Pueblo of San Juan there was stress over the problem of possibilities of some individuals being able to reap personal gain from the site. There was also concern about further excavation with its chance of disturbing more burials, though their major disturbance had resulted from use of bulldozers by San Juan members who had intended using the land for adobe-making and/or agriculture in the 1940s.

The outcome? In the face of disagreements within San Juan itself, nothing could be done. The proposed plans were dropped, and with ten years Onate's dream city once more was lost to most people, its story, its artifacts, even its shape a shadow.

The site of San Gabriel del Yungue (A.D. 1250 or 1300 – 1610) originally was that of an old and once flourishing pueblo, Yungue. From the literature we know that it became the first Spanish town in New Mexico which, in the sixteenth – seventeenth centuries, included today's Arizona. We also know that it represents the second oldest European settlement in what now is the United States and once could and should have been neatly excavated and restored, like eighteenth century colonial Williamsburg, Virgina, where in a day thousands of visitors glimpse for a few hours the life and conditions known to our early English settlers. But the few visitors who set out to see San Gabriel del Yungue today complain that nothing is visible except for some cultivated fields and two occupied dwellings, one, very modern, atop the highest mound of the old village and the other where the stubs of walls once making up the south mound (if there was one) remain hidden by an old adobe home with its outbuildings.

Archaeology's first step toward the rescue of history (sisters under the skin) in the widely important matter of location of San Gabriel del Yungue was when Bandelier rode his horse onto the scene (or was he on foot, as so often?) sometime between 1880 and 1885), talked with the San Juan elders and thus located and sketched the ruin of New Mexico's first capital, still known in native tradition. His explanation that it often was confused with Chamita, a short distance up the Chama, is explained in our present knowledge that the surface of old Yungue was occupied from the late 1880s by Spanish-Americans, some of whose ancestors conceivably may have been descendants of Onate's colonists.

Technically they were squatters on Indian land and in the 1920s were ordered to leave both by the council of San Juan Pueblo and by the newly created U.S. Pueblo Lands Board.

But Bandelier's answer to the question of precisely where and just what "Yungue" was (also recorded as "Yunque Yunque" and in other elaborated variations which the San Juan Indians today claim should have been correctly and simply "Yungue Ouinge," meaning "the place known as Yungue"), was not entirely satisfactory to the historians. There also was the problem of what its relation had been to San Juan Bautista, the still existent Pueblo named by Onate himself. And if the Spaniards settled in San Gabriel del Yungue (often but not always written merely as "San Gabriel"), how could they also dateline some of their messages to officials in Mexico as from "San Juan"?

The intermitten tale of archaeology-to-the-rescue begun by Bandelier's late 19th century investigations was taken up in 1944 when Marjorie Tichy, curator of archaeology for the Museum of New Mexico in Santa Fe, was asked by Dr. Edgar L. Hewett, director of that Museum, to go out to San Juan Pueblo and learn what was under way. Rumor had it that major adobe-making was being handled by some of the Pueblo men along the tops and rises of the old mounds of the ruin identified as Yunque. Nothing produces better adobes than the walls of old ruins in which adobe has been used but, in such procedure, the ruins necessarily cease to exist.

As a result of this visit, Tichy was permitted to set up a one week excavation to be carried on by herself and two persons, a native man and wife, toward the south end of the old west house mound. Little came from this abbreviated dig except the renewed conviction that the site fitted the criteria for Yungue.

A few months earlier, Steve Trujillo, one of the San Juan men, in crossing the field near Tichy's excavation had chanced to kick up a curved piece of bronze on which a raised design decorated the exterior. Realizing the possibility of its importance, he turned it over to a much interested friend from Santa Fe. The friend promptly passed it on to Tichy, and she in turn sent it to one of the major American specialists on colonial Spanish artifacts. The opinion he returned was that it could have been part of the bell in the San Gabriel Church (an opinion since partly countered by others who belived it be broken from one of the metal mortars for grinding herbs and medicines, such as we know Onate had with him) and definitely was of the Spanish Colonial period.

Then, in 1946, word reached Santa Fe that a bulldozer was

12

being used to cut down parts of the old mounds at San Juan in a new adobe-makng project. Taking another museum employee as a companion, Tichy went to San Juan and found, alas, that the story had not been exaggerated. Moreover, in walking over the dusty top-soil, they found masses of human bones and potsherds which had been brought to the surface by the bulldozer. They also found a chunk of corroded metal which turned out to be a section of chain mail, rusted together but definitely identifiable!

The Museum now notified the Bureau of Indian Affairs in Albuqueruqe, asking for aid. The Bureau sent out a man to discuss the problem with the Governor of San Juan Pueblo, explaining the importance of this historic site to Indians and non-Indians alike. The Governor, who happened to own the land involved, in turn explained that the Indians had not understood the matter before, and he promised that in the future, before any appreciable adobe making or cultivation was done there, the BIA would be advised.

Then, in 1951 Jose Abeita, one of the elderly San Juan leaders, while digging adobe from the side of the old west mound to make into adobe bricks for his daughter's home (on top of that mound) found that he had struck and broken a native type stone griddle at the bottom of his pit. Beneath the stone had been a cooking vessel, now likewise broken. Nested inside that vessel he saw what he thought must be "an old hat."

Wondering — correctly — whether that strange object might not be of some importance, he took it to Henry Kramer, owner of the local general store, who "gave him something for it" and at once carried it to Marjorie Tichy (now Lambert) at the state Museum. She promptly sent the "hat" to Harold L. Peterson, primary American authority on armor, and was rewarded with the statement that it had been a flat type archer's helmet and was not only the oldest piece of armor ever found in the United States but had been fashioned in Europe a century before Onate had brought his colony into New Mexico. It must have been purchased by that leader with a collection of secondhand armor which he had had to order in large lots for the volunteer "soldier settlers" who lacked some or all of their own required equipment for the expedition. At the time the "helmet" was found all the iron had disappeared from its metal. Thus it was merely a shape composed of iron rust and hence exceedingly fragile. Extensive conservation treatment by the Museum of New Mexico since, however, has provided enough stability so that the piece could be exhibited on special occasions.

We can regret that permission and funds were not raised for

an extensive program of excavation at Yungue during this period of few but extraordinary finds. Instead, eight years passed quietly, and then, in the early spring of 1959, I received a letter from the then Governor of San Juan Pueblo requesting that, as head of the University of New Mexico's Archaeological Field School for that summer session of six weeks, I should bring our crew (usually forty to sixty) of student excavtors plus six student assistant overseers — and "find out what San Juan had!" It was the first time any Pueblo had ever made a request for archaeological work on their lands, and we hastily changed our tentative summer plans to accommodate this important assignment.

One of our first pieces of preparation, other than checking adequate field equipment to be used by students and the scattering of San Juan men we hoped to hire for aid with some of the heavier tasks, was a quick review of Hammond and Rey's two volume *Onate, the Colonizer of New Mexico*, the fullest reference on this site. (In order to minimize bulk,) we have not here given page references to these two volumes; they are multitudinous.) The other source we wanted to check at once was the traditional history of Yungue as a unit in the San Juan complex, as carried down from the past by the San Juan elders. Yungue definitely had been a part of San Juan, yes. But what was its actual relationship to that other section, Okeh, also a part of San Juan? The main plaza of each had been no more than one-fourth mile apart from that of the other, in a straight line.

Lambert's brief work and the finds by the Indians had proved that the site known to the Indians as Yungue quite certainly had been Onate's San Gabriel. But what had it been before Onate arrived?

According to tradition, said the elders of San Juan Pueblo, two branches of Tewa-speaking ancestors had come out of the northwest in prehistoric times. One, its members all classified as Summer People, settled for some years at various sites in the Chama Valley. The other, classified as Winter People, after having come out of the northwest wandered for some years east of the Sangre de Cristo Mountains on the edge of the Plains and then came down the east side of the Rio Grande Valley. Details in tradition are not of serious concern in our studies, but general lines of movement may offer leads.

In the meantime, some of the Summer People were leaving the Chama and its tributaries to resettle along the west bank of the Rio Grande. As time passed, the Summer and the Winter People

14

redistributed themselves so that every Tewa Pueblo had a group of each. The pueblo of Yungue was one of the villages on the western edge of the Rio Grande settled during the prehistoric period by Summer People who had moved down the Chama Valley. It is not difficult for an archaeologist to place an approximate date on this move. Tree-ring records indicate that the upper Rio Grande, like the Four Corners area, suffered increasing drought during the 1200s, especially through the second half of that century. Checking for the earliest types of pottery present in Yungue, we found Santa Fe and Wiyo Black-on-whites, characteristically indicative of the second half of the A.D. 1200s and running into the 1300s in this region.

One of the settlement patterns we have been able to spot for this stage was the amalgamation of some of the smaller Pueblos into single larger Pueblos (in some cases very large) during the A.D. 1250-1350 period. Such sites would have had the manpower to put in ditches for irrigation. The best locations for such sites were on tributaries where an appreciable natural drop carried water toward some larger stream. That drop made it possible to get the water out onto the potential farm land bordering the tributary without requiring such long ditches as would be necessary to raise water from a big stream with a slight drop, such as the Rio Grande, onto possible farm land along its banks. Our first example of this was noted at the ancestral Tewa pueblo of Sapawe (Ellis 1970), and irrigation ditches of this period since have been reported from a number of other ancestral Tewa pueblos in the Chama drainage and similarly in the Nambe area and farther down the Rio Grande.

The last of the Tewa moves from the Chama into the upper Rio Grande and similarly into the eastern foothills of the Sangre de Cristo Mountains must have dated from the late 1500s. At that time, as we know from tree ring records, such a lengthy drought struck the Pajarito Plateau and the adjoining Chama area that this entire high territory was abandoned. The people joined their relatives in the Rio Grande bottom, especially where tributaries, such as the Chama, the Nambe, and lower Santa Clara Creek, and some other tributaries on both sides of the Rio Grande provided water and valley or delta land to be planted.

San Juan tradition places one of the units of Winter People as first settling some miles above present San Juan Pueblo but below the opening to Taos Cañon. When their pueblo and their fields were washed out by flood, the inhabitants of that site moved down river and rebuilt. Once again their village was ruined by a flood.

This time they went to the people of Yungue, still farther south, and asked if they might resettle themselves across from that pueblo, on the bluff above the eastern edge of the river. Yungue agreed to that arrangement, and the new village still known as Okeh thus was established. Surface sherds suggest that this event occurred in the 1300s. The close proximity of the two peoples led to their becoming "like brothers" and they decided to merge into a single tribe though living in two communities about one-fourth mile apart. The ritual head of the Summer people would be the chief priest responsible for all activities pertaining to the summer ceremonial sequence (concentrating especially, but not solely, on the growth of domesticated plants) and would be the principal tribal leader during that period. In a parallel arrangement, the ritual head of the Winter people would be the winter chief and responsible for all activities pertaining to the winter ceremonial sequence, concentrating especially, but not solely, on fertility of animals, wild and domestic. Eventually, it is said, many of the Summer people from Yungue moved to join the Winter people living on the bluff at Okeh. Thus Okeh became the larger settlement.

There is no problem in Pueblo thought with the fact that a *Pueblo* is understood not to be an architectural unit (as commonly supposed by non-Indians), but is a *tribe* living in one or several such architectural units which may be thought of as parallel to apartment houses or even more closely to condominiums. For example, the visitor notes that Taos Pueblo has two easily visible "pueblos," architectural units, one on each side of the stream. Today's Laguna Pueblo is a single tribe with a single center, Old Laguna, but it has some nine or more villages or pueblos in which the tribesmen live on Laguna land.[1] Understanding that a Pueblo tribe may be made up of several geographic units, though the whole comprises one sociological unit, is important.

So we must picture our sixteenth century San Juan tribe as occupying two geographic centers, very close to each other and with a part of their farms separated only by the stream of the Rio Grande. At least the Yungue people were also cultivating the delta

1. *Note: we use the non-capitalized form for the architectural unit but the capitalized form, Pueblo, for the tribe, for the village name, for an individual member of any Pueblo tribe, and for the culture characteristic of Pueblo tribes. Some but not all of the smaller pueblos belonging to a tribe began as farm sites at a distance out from the main village.*

the expedition) reached San Gabriel, the new capital, on Christmas eve, 1600.

The general statement that the move of Onate's headquarters and of the Spaniards in general from Okeh to Yungue during the midwinter period of 1600-1601 appears to be safe.

Certainly that move could not have been made in a day — but why was it made at all? Therein hangs a tale of human beings with their pressing desires, habits, and customs — some of the most prominent sectors of what the anthropologist refers to as the "culture" of a people.

If we return to the long and hard trek northward from Mexico, we recall that Onate and his captains, impatient at the necessary slowness of the main party traveling with eighty-three loaded ox-carts and wagons and driving over 7000 horses, cattle, sheep, goats, and even pigs, hastened ahead of the burdened settlers. After introducing themselves at San Juan, they spent some four weeks visiting and explaining themselves and their mission to Pueblos not encountered on their route. The next venture recorded is their beginning work on an irrigation ditch system at San Juan which was to serve "the city of our father San Francisco." We are told nothing more concerning these ditches except that some 1500 of the local Indians were giving the Spaniards a hand. Considering that Tewa ancestors had been managing ditch irrigation with stone implements for the last 300 years and that the Spaniards' metal implements all were on the ox carts in transit, it is probable that the natives would have been considerably more adept than the Spanish captains at handling the task.

Reading farther, we learn that as soon as the group of soldier-colonists did arrive at San Juan, they constructed a church which within two weeks was complete enough for the Spaniards to stage its dedicaton mass. The only type of structure which could have been raised here in that time period, large enough to hold some 500 persons, and possibly more if we consider that Indian leaders may have been invited as guests, would have been of jacal, vertical posts set into a trench and plastered inside and out with mud. Such structures are not costly in time or labor but their lifetime is limited, and we note that no one ever has reported finding remains of this first and impermanent church. Its site probably has been built over once and again since its abandonment almost four centuries ago.

There is no further mention of that "city of our father San Francisco." As one of the witnesses later explained, the colonists

over →

of the Chama. Whether the combined tribe had a name we do not know; we do know that Onate conferred the patron saint and the name "San Juan Bautista," to the combined tribe as such. Onate's occasional use of the term "San Juan de los Caballeros" (San Juan of the Gentlemen) presumably refers to the kindly cooperative arrangement by the tribesmen in permitting the Spaniards, upon their arrival, to move in with local families or, more likely, to take over temporarily empty houses, of which some always exist in a pueblo. The two geographic divisions of the tribe, more or less comparable to our named geographic sections of cities or towns, have continued to retain their local names, Okeh and Yungue, even to the present, though "Yungue" is rarely heard today because of the few tribesmen presently living in that district. "San Juan" has been used to cover the major area of use by all San Juan people as well as for the village of Okeh throughout American times. This probably was true in Spanish Colonial times was well, thus explaining Captain Velasco's commentary in a letter to the viceroy, March 22, 1601, sent out from San Gabriel, that in first reaching northern New Mexico

> ... We came to a pueblo, where the governor ordered a halt. It is
> the one from which I am writing your lordship. We have been
> here three years ...

Hammond and Rey 1953:609

We would say that Velasco was referring to the Spaniards by 1601 having been in the San Juan area, (Okeh and Yungue together with their environs) for three years, even as we ourselves commonly combine the two closely adjoining sites under the single geographic term of "San Juan."

The problem of whether the Spaniards actually did move into Okeh at first and later took over Yungue, or settled in Yungue at the beginning and remained there, has puzzled historians. Hammond and Rey, carefully sorting over the Onate papers, came to the conclusion that as all communications sent out from New Mexico between the summer of 1598 and February 15, 1599 had been datelined as written from San Juan, whereas all letters and/or reports datelined between March 22, 1601 and October 1601 were sent out as from San Gabriel, it would appear that San Juan (Okeh) had been Onate's first headquarters but that between the spring of 1599 and March of 1601 the Spaniards had taken over Yungue on a permanent basis. We know that Onate's second group of "soldier-colonialists" (those recruited after the first group left Mexico, in order to make up the number of persons guaranteed by Onate for had refused to put out the labor necessary for constructing a town because they found life here too full of privations and did not want to remain in New Mexico. True, the trek up from Mexico had been rough and food scarce. Onate, as governor, quite obviously had planned a "city" from the beginning, one where the extra coaches he had brought could be driven and at least some houses would have beds with silken spreads and there would be occasions for wearing one's best dress clothing. But certainly mixing and laying adobes for several hundred houses unquestionably would have taken a large block of time. Moreover, the problem of using only semi-satisfactory cottonwood for roof beams or of cutting pines and bringing them out of the mountains, quite possibly involving dangers from Indians as well as months of labor, would have greatly reduced the time available for putting in family farms — and the all important pursuit of some possible source of riches.

Previously, every Spanish expedition into this area had been exploratory with the preliminary hope of finding an easily available source of wealth. Even after the members of the expedition had returned, empty-handed, to Mexico, alluring tales concerning what some thought might have been found had there been more time persisted. Onate's "colonists" were not moving into the Southwest long enough after those explorers had left it for their interests to have become very enthusiastically concentrated on agriculture or on house building. Apparently this problem had not occurred to Onate, nor, we would surmise, to any of the other prominent Spanish leaders who had competed for the position of leading the first group of colonists into this fairly distant frontier. It was a built-in hazard.

But many of the men had brought wives and families and apart from Onate's personal desire that his group should have at least a settlement of their own, the colonists were complaining all too audibly at living in native houses where ventilation from the smoky fires of cottonwood brought from the valley groves was almost nil, and bedbugs and other biting insects could not be overlooked as sources of discomfort.

How much do we know of Pueblo living conditions for the late pre-Spanish period? If the Spaniards were to give up construction of a town, in exchange for renovation of an already standing pueblo, what could they expect that native-built structure to be like?

By the 1500s, many pueblos were made up of one or more house blocks, the arrangement of which was fitted to the contours

19

of the location chosen for the village. Some consisted of house blocks arranged around a rectangular central plaza or two plazas in which were one or more great underground kivas to accommodate major religious and secular functions involving all or a large part of the tribe. There also were varied numbers of smaller kivas in which meetings of the diversified religious societies in which membership might consist of a few or many individuals were held. As in our own cities and towns, all parts of a village were not necessarily in good condition at any one time; some houses were closed and fell into ruins after families died out.

We were fortunate in having a description of Yungue by Villagra in *History of New Mexico*, 1610 (Canto xxvii, fol. 228), eventually to be quoted by Bandelier (1892:59:fn 1). Villagra gave Yungue but one plaza, rectangular and with an entrance at each corner which he said the Spaniards themselves put in after they had fortified it with field stones and muskets. (Elsewhere we read that no fortifications as such were added.) The houses and the terraces of flat house roofs were high, a statement which Bandelier interprets as referring to two or three stories of rooms. In spite of his statement (Bandelier 1892:59) that "all had disappeared" by the time he visited the site, he provides a simple map (Plate 2, Fig. 10) showing two house blocks, each with a rough right angle bend toward its center, possibly indicative of where the ends of two smaller house blocks came close together or met. At what would have been the other two corners, openings were indicated.

A Pueblo home usually was part of a house block. Each family might construct its own apartment as a addition to others already present, but some house blocks were laid up in large units in which parallel walls were built as long as the house block was planned to be and cross walls then were set between those walls to cut off individual rooms or apartments. A Pueblo apartment in a large site of the late prehistoric and early historic period quite commonly was three rooms deep, its front facing onto a plaza and the back being either a solid outer wall or a wall which served as back not only to the apartment just described but also to a similar one facing in the opposite direction. Such long walls would have been put together by Pueblo men under the planned direction of certain of the Pueblo's officers. In 1892 Bandelier found Santo Domingo Pueblo laying up new long walls in this fashion for house blocks intended to replace those which had recently disappeared in a flood. The cross walls were put in by the individual families who would own their apartments. This appears to have been the system earlier used in building the great Chaco Pueblos of northwestern New Mexico and a great many others, whether of masonry or, as so commonly in the Rio Grande valley, of coursed adobe. And this is the system we found had been used in building the native house blocks of Yungue Pueblo.

The entrance to Pueblo rooms characteristically was by means of a ladder which descended at a slight slope through a hatchway in the roof. The roof also was reached by ladder; drawing up the ladders for centuries had been a means of protection from enemies. Smoke from the floor firepit used for cooking and heating was expected to find its slow way upward for escape through the same hatchway in the roof. Chimneys and corner fireplaces which today's Southwesterners so often think of as characteristically "Pueblo," actually were of Spanish introduction.

If a pueblo house block was to be two or more stories high, the upper stories must be terraced back so that the roof hatchway which served as smoke hole and ladder accessway would not be in the floor of a living room directly above. Otherwise, the room with the hatchway in its floor would be filled with smoke whenever someone built a fire in the firepit of the lower room. It seems that in large house blocks first floor rooms quite commonly were used only for storage if there were living rooms directly above.

The secular architecture which produced the Pueblo home was the most highly developed of any north of Mexico, but in order to fit Spanish tastes, some modifications clearly would be necessary. Of primary importance were floor level doorways and a few windows, probably small and left uncovered in summer but possibly filled in with a slab of translucent selenite or, more likely, with wood in winter.

What to do?

One obviously could not make over the dwelling of one's host — but if the Spaniards could only arrange to acquire old Yungue, part of it moldering in the sun but part still occupied — ?

The majority of the Indians still living there just might be persuaded to cross the Rio Grande and move in with their relatives at Okeh — leaving a few whose labors would be engaged in the renovations and repair of Yungue to something approaching Spanish specifications. At least the Spanish elite and the families as such thus could be accommodated with fair comfort. Perhaps one considerable section of rooms might be left relatively unchanged for use as barracks to house the unmarried soldier-settlers. Some walls probably would need stabilizing or replacing. A small block of adjoining rooms might be modified and arranged with an adjoining room into some approximation of a Spanish kitchen to serve the five or six religious brothers as their monastery. Near the church, of course, for an adequate and permanent church must be raised in a prominent spot as soon as possible.

And thus it was done.

As archaeologists, we read the dream (which no one had time or felt the need to record in those last days of the 1500s) through its accomplishment. Today's San Juan people knew from their ancestors only that the old west mound had served the Spaniards as barracks, and some told various interested inquirers that the church was said to have stood somewhere toward the south side of what could be made out of the general layout of the ruins today. Beneath the Martinez house south of the little access road? Or at one side? Or in their field?

Our only approximate map of the whole original site, as we have indicated, is that sketched by Bandelier, which in general is born out by aerial photographs and ground shots taken after our excavations, though these modern depictions can show only what was left after the modifications engendered by 19th-20th century changes planned by the natives for economic "improvements."

We began our excavations a few feet north of the front porch of the house on the west mound with permission of the owners but with a warning that their intention was to shortly expand their establishment in all directions. By the following season, the area in front of that porch might become a swimming pool or a rose garden. In other words, any investigation planned must be done at once or given up.

Our entire first season (1959) was spent on uncovering the northern half of what was left of the west mound, both edges as well as the upper surface having been cut into by removal of an unknown number of cubic feet of soil by use of a bulldozer. What we learned was that this mound had been constructed and used in four successive stages. And we should add that in spite of what obviously was now gone from the two sides of the west mound at field (Plaza) level, it was quite certain that all the stages ever existent still were represented. Some but not a great deal of soil had been intentionally cut away from the upper surface of this mound, as had been admitted and as we already have described, but considerably more probably had disappeared through erosion between the period of occupation by Onate's men (early 1600s) and its reoccupation, with new and different structures, by Spanish-

22

Americans between the late 1800s and the early 1920s.

The bulldozer cuts and adobe pits at the edges of the mound had left only partial walls to the outermost rooms which our excavations uncovered. We cannot state with any certainty just how many rooms would have been present in an original cross-section of the main portion of this mound. We do know that the first construction and occupation here dated from the mid A.D. 1200s or early 1300s as indicated by sherds of Santa Fe and Wiyo Black-on-white. However, as in all the Yungue areas in which we excavated, the breaking down of old walls and consequent disturbance of fill in upper rooms and especially of fill which came to be deposited in later-built or later-renovated rooms, had resulted in mixing of sherds known to actually represent different periods. Therefore, except for noting the generally understood date range on sherds present, and their comparative proportions by type, data from sherd complexes could provide little information. Old vessels, even if cracked or otherwise disfigured sometimes were buried in a corner of the floor of first floor rooms for holding food materials, probably ground corn flour or shelled corn, comfortably at hand for meal planners.

The early rooms had been built with coursed adobe walls laid up in layered courses of adobe patted into place, the initial course lying directly on native soil, a custom discarded by the second period. A firepit or rectangular box had been cut into the native soil, usually toward the east wall. The floor and pit both were finished with adobe plaster.

Such a pit provided both heat and cooking facilities, and directly above it an opening would have been left in the roof, a sturdily edged hatchway to serve both as an exit for the smoke and an entryway for the ladder up and down which the householders climbed as we would use a stairway. Via this ladder they could reach the second story, though probably, if the lower floor was used for cooking, the hatchway would open onto one of the open areas of the roof to one side of the second story living rooms, thus avoiding, as we explained earlier, the problem of smoke from the fire in a first story room venting directly into a living room above. This was the major reason why pueblos of more than one story characteristically were planned with set-backs for the upper rooms. On the unroofed open floor space provided by those set-backs would be not only the hatchway opening for the room below but also a fire hearth for open-air cooking in good weather, an area for drying corn after harvest, and even sufficient space for sleeping

23

out on hot summer nights and handling food preparation or working on pottery making, basketry, or other tasks until the winter
chill set in. Such an open terrace arrangement could almost double
one's usable house area.

How would we know that most of the lower floor rooms in this
structure and in many other pueblos of this period in the northern
Southwest were intended for storage? When there is neither firepit
nor firebox in the floor of the first story, we can be quite certain
the rooms of that level would have been too cold for winter occupation, though they would have served well for storage those of the
next story above were intended for living and sleeping quarters
and also for corn grinding and cooking.

Floor level doorways were considered dangerous even into the
historic period and hence were almost unknown except in some of
the cliff dwellings or between inner rooms and sometimes into a
courtyard, if the entire pueblo was walled except for protected
openings. A householder could climb his ladder onto the second
floor and pull it up after himself if he wanted no one else to follow
him. Other ladders went on to upper stories.

To judge from our excavations, even the lower floor rooms of
Yungue were not usually connected to each other by doorway
openings; most rooms must have had a ladder reaching down from
above.

How many stories the west mound house block had we could
not determine with complete certainty. There was clear evidence
of a second floor having been constructed, the walls of this and of
later-added stories being of coursed adobe laid upon a cobblestone
foundation usually two stones wide and one or two deep. This
makes us quite sure that the structure originally had been only one
story high, and that by the time it was decided to add a second
story, the use of a cobble foundation had become popular.

Eventually, in a third stage, some of the old walls were cut
down, probably with renewal repairs in mind. The debris from
their upper parts was spread as fill on which to lay a new floor, and
fresh walls were raised either directly on the stubs of the old walls
or at a slightly different angle, the base being the knocked-down
and probably tamped soil from the older walls.

Here we find ourselves uncovering a major job of reconstruction which we can summarize as consisting of the upper part of the
original bottom or first story walls being cut off and the debris
used to fill in the room outline. A new set of walls then was constructed on the butts of the old walls as bases or directly on the fill

in those cases where a slightly different wall orientation now was followed. In both, parallel walls evidently had been laid up by groups of men working under planned direction. These newer rooms, representing a second period of occupation of the west mound, may have been occupied by the last of the Yungue Pueblo people to live here and then was merely cleared by native workers in accord with Onate's concept of adapting the west mound to serve as barracks for his single men. Or this may have been a renovation project intended to make an old portion of the west mound habitable for the colonists by knocking down a block of unstable walls and roofs and having them largely replaced on the old bases. No detail on renovation of any of the house blocks is mentioned in Spanish papers.

But, interestingly because this is a point rarely thought of in relation to the housing of Spanish soldiers, the first (bottom) floor rooms quite certainly were not the actual living quarters. The renovated lower story would have served primarily for storage, as we known from the lack of firepits or fireboxes. Above those rooms was the second story, consisting of living quarters. This we know from the fact that when the house block collapsed some time after Yungue was abandoned by the Spaniards, being moved by their new leader to Santa Fe (1610), the debris from this second story fell into the vacant rooms below. It was in this fill that we found numerous fragments of iron and bronze, too small, broken, and corroded to be recognizable as parts of specific artifacts but obviously of Spanish introduction. In this debris there also were four sherds of the highly tin-glazed and colorful 16th century maiolica, probably made in Mexico and brought from there as part of the men's living equipment.

The only whole artifacts we found in this association were two small brass cups made to fit into each other, the type of container into which small amounts of gold dust or other valuable material could be placed for weighing on one of the old type balance scales. Some young man had hopefully included them in his baggage from Mexico but left them when none of the wished-for wealth could be located.

The replacing of much of the old walls here, and the finishing of the new ones with a fresh coat of adobe plaster would have greatly minimized the problem of bedbugs, formerly not unusual in old pueblo structures, those of Spanish-American villagers, and even in some of the town homes of New Mexico as late as into the edge of the 1940's. Those unwelcome creatures were said to be

25

present in part of the local timber even as it was brought from the forests, and until the development of DDT during World War II, their elimination from rooms with viga ceilings could be very difficult. New Mexico was not alone. I well recall the annual spring spraying of an apartment owned by the University of Chicago when I lived in that apartment as well as using it as a laboratory and classroom while teaching for the University.

We found very few instances in which the upper or the lower floor rooms of the west mound appeared to have opened into each other.

Only a few inches below the present surface of the west mound, we came across remnants of the clay floors (often whitewashed) of Spanish-American dwellings which had been constructed between the late 1800s (or before) and approximately 1920, when the natives of San Juan began a campaign to persuade those families, as trespassers, to move off Indian land. This movement was brought to a head with the decisions of the San Juan Council and also of the Pueblo Lands Board in the 1920s and early 1930s.

In holes which evidently once had been root cellars or merely trash pits cut down into the filled rooms of colonial Spanish period, we found old shoes, bottles, pieces from farm implements, and in some cases secondary burials, usually but not always of infants and children, the bones sometimes folded into newspapers dating from our own lifetime. Evidently later occupants of this mound (Spanish-Americans), like our own excavators, had come across the burials while building their own structures in the upper levels on the mound and at least in some cases had reintered them. As we would learn at the end of this summer and during our work of the following season at the upper end of the east mound, this entire site, or at least the mounds as such, had been utilized as a burying ground after the Spanish colonists had left and evidently before use of the Catholic churchyard as a cemetery had been accepted by the natives.

Our work on the east mound (we skipped whatever remained of the north mound because of growing concern for probable time limitations) began in the north portion, just south of Lee Montoya's fence, in late 1959 and was continued in 1960. Nowhere could one see any signs of walls on the surface. Examination of a now much broken down cut for an irrigation ditch which had carried water southward into a former corn field just north of the little access road, showed that it had led through a heavily used burial plot, in part apparently an old ash pile but in part the fill of rooms after their abandonment by the Spaniards. It also had been, as we were told, the location of one of the 20th century adobe-mixing pits. We staked off "sections" or "areas" where we could work downward and sideways until we should locate some room walls to provide a natural and expandable grid indicating the general layout of this house block.

Alignment for the rooms toward the north end of the east mound, as for those of the west mound, was more or less north-south, but variations in line suggest that they had been built by family groups, perhaps over a period of a few years rather than as a planned whole. Their fill contained plentiful sherds, charcoal, ash, some stone, a few animal bones, and a scattering of broken stone and bone implements. Evidently, like the west mound, the east mound originally had been at least two stories high. The first story rooms were largely devoid of fireboxes and hence quite surely had been intended for storage, and the debris now filling the roofless room outlines to a depth of several feet could have come only from collapsed upper stories, the living quarters. That the Spaniards had occupied these quarters definitely was indicated by scattered finds of corroded metal fragments and even a few maiolica sherds, as in the west mound.

But the north end of the east mound had no more been the *center* of the Spanish "city" than had the west mound. Where were the headquarters of Onate and his captains, certain to have been modified to more closely fit Spanish standards of that day? And the apartments for the 42 to 50 families of lesser status? And that church of San Miguel in which, as we read in the Hammond and Rey papers, on Spetember 7, 1601, the dissident colonists, fearful of the drastic food shortage in the drought years of 1600-1601, discontented at lack of any visible ways to make quick personal fortunes, bored by shortage of unmarried Spanish women, and carrying the prejudice of a Spanish cultural heritage condemning agriculture as one of the lowest of all occupations, plus, for the clerics, conviction that the type of treatment received by the Pueblos in pillaging and punishment by the Spaniards was keeping the number of conversions low — met while Onate was out on the Plains with a party — and decided to desert and make the best possible time back to Mexico? And where on October 2, 1601, the 23 remaining loyal colonists met to compose documents stating their approval of Onate's leadershp, the fertility of the land, and their ardent desire to remain at San Gabriel?

Counting the weeks still covered by our excavation permit, we decided to skip two or three rows of the houses we had been following southward, that area to be caught up, we hoped, in some later uncovering. Our thought was to start an experimental trench toward the center of a now flat field, long Lee Montoya's corn patch, in what presumably should have been the mid section of the east mound. Years of ditch irrigation had hardened the soil, impregnated as it was with the clay of once existent house walls.

To our delight, within the first day we found walls, or at least their stubs which fortunately had been just far enough below the bulldozer line and the plow line to be saved. Excitement began to rise as we followed those bases, ranging from a few inches to over a foot in height, for they opened up a new vision of row after row of contiguous rooms stretching from what had been the eastern limits of this house mass all the way to what had been the eastern edge of the big central plaza. (See 1962 map.) But it was as we uncovered the southeastern corner of this big rectangular structure that enthusiasm really began to soar.

For there, at last, we definitely could recognize the apartments which had been renovated for Spanish use, rooms opened into each other by means of floor level doorways. Whatever the doors had been, a suspended hide or the old Spanish type wooden door with heavy extended pegs at top and bottom of one margin to fit into cups cut into possibly once existent wooden lintels, no evidence remains today. We may guess, from the few comments in the Onate papers, that small windows similarly were cut through some of the outer walls to aid with the problem of ventilation, though none of the walls now remaining were high enough to show such features.

Some of the "apartments" (VI, IV, I) found as we approached the southeast corner of this house block were represented by but onc first story room with a ground floor doorway opening onto the space separating the eastern edge of this house block from the old peripheral mound of debris where deposits from the Spanish period were combined with those from preceding times rather than providing a neat and different top layer. The Spanish debris, resulting from their short occupation of 9 years, certainly should have been minimal in comparison to that of the earlier native occupation of some three hundred years but the admitted bulldozing had, as everywhere in Yungue, mixed the materials rather than eliminating either.

As elsewhere, if no firepit was found in the ground floor of a southeast apartment, we had to surmise that the first story room had served for storage as well as an entry chamber and that the living quarters, with cooking facilities, had been above, on the second story. This one ground floor room type with outside doorway we classified, on the basis of what we could see, as "one room apartments." In reality, they must have had two rooms, at least: a living-cooking room, and possibly one or more adjoining rooms above the bottom story entry-storage room.

There also were some two ground floor room apartments (VII, V) near the southeastern corner of this house block, with a doorway opening between those rooms and the exterior. (See Plan of Yungue Spanish Area, 1960.) One would suppose that the living quarters on the second floor of these had consisted of at least two rooms, one behind the other. For these the original Pueblo style apartments would have required no changes except for cutting Spanish type doorways into the walls, strengthening or replacing some walls as needed, and probably covering all the interior with a new layer of smooth adobe plaster.

But it was the second and the fourth apartments, around the corner, fronting on the south side of this house block that really captured our imagination. The second (II) consisted of a long narrow room (C) with three doorways, one leading in from the exterior, one opening into adjoining room M, behind C and similar to it but longer, and one connecting with room B, on the east side of C, almost equally long and slightly wider than C. A pottery vessel buried to its neck for storage use was found against one wall in room B and another in C. But these were not the most important finds here. Just inside the outer door, opposite the jar, was a low cobblestone "table," approximately 4 inches high, 2 feet long, and only slightly less in width. Toward the northern corner of this same room was a second cobblestone "table" of the same proportions except for a slight addition in length. Directly and close in front of it was a Spanish (non-plastered) firepit in the floor, and against the north end of the "table" a locally made micaceous ware cooking jar stood upright in a slight depression in the floor. Plentiful ash was scattered over and around the "table," firepit, and jar.

It was the association of cooking jar, firepit, "table," and that considerable distribution of ash which provided the clue we needed. This had been not merely a room but an area for cooking. The firepit made that clear, and there were two more firepits of similar type in the room adjoining to the north.

Where had we seen something like the cobble "table" before,

though with an adobe-plastered surface — and from two or three to ten times as long? Of course: in the special miniature outside rooms some of the more conservative Rio Grande Pueblo families still use for preparing foods on ceremonial occasions but which also are found on larger scale in special rooms similarly used to cook meals for Pueblo religious societies when in retreat. The old Cushing and Stevenson reports show pictures of such "cooking shelves," as I have been calling them but which those older anthropologists referred to as "cooking fireplaces introduced by the Spaniards" (or some approximation of that phrase) on which a series of small fires burn beneath stone griddles or vessels supported by stone "fire dogs." The smoke from that extended hearth was picked up and carried off by a hood extending down from the roof and topped with several European cooking hearths in Spanish period Yungue; there may have been only the old Pueblo type open hatchway, with a draft aided by the nearby doorway. But Spanish introduction of the raised cobblestone hearths for cooking at this time seems certain.

Another introduction by the Spaniards was the dome outdoor oven for baking bread and other pastries of the wheat flour they ground in the village mill. Raised above the ground by a platform a few inches high, simply made of cobbles held in adobe and topped by a dome of clay with an opening at the base and vent hole above, it was heated by a fire built inside. The ashes and charcoal then swept out and the door opening closed with a slab after the goods to be baked had been set inside. The remains of five of these, the earliest known for our Southwest, were found in front of some of the east and southeast apartments.

Two room apartment VIII, immediately to the north of II, had no special features other than evidence of eight roof supports having been installed against the two west walls, supposedly because the Spaniards found those walls fragile.

The next apartment, III, to the west of II, had three large first story rooms, all connected by floor level doorways, but we found no clear evidence of cooking facilities. One pottery vessel had been left buried in the northern and one in the southern room (E and K), and a one-metate bin for corn grinding still stood in the central room, J. These rooms may have had shallow Spanish-type firepits; some of the floors were irregular enough to leave us in doubt. Or such rooms could have served for storage of the great list of items brought to New Mexico for colony usage, a mass requiring space and easy access. But note: our guesses in this line definitely are no more than that.

Adjoining apartment III on the west was a collection for four small rooms (X: F and I; XI: G; and XII: II), as well as big room P, with firepit. Three of these were connected by doorways. Unfortunately, one notes that at the western edge there is a slight discrepancy between the 1960 map of "Yungue Spanish Area" and that marked "Yungue, Summer 1962." The problem, we believe, lies in the 1960 map, made before excavation was completed, representing rooms G and II as two separate cubicles, each tying in, via a doorway, to an adjoining small room on the west. The 1962 map showing those "adjoining rooms" as one long room, part of the two room southwest corner apartment, appears to be correct, but it is quite possible that both floor plans had been used, in successive periods.

Then, just to the south of this room complex, not connected to any other room but with an outside entrance of its own, we uncovered apartment XIII, a remarkable one room "kitchen complex" with its own two divisions separated, primarily, by two "cobble hearths." Here was by far the most elaborately arranged functioning unit encountered anywhere in this site.

The outside entrance to this room, on the west, led into what may have been a small store room. To one's right, on passing from this small room through the doorway into the main room, was a long "cobble hearth," a bit more than half the length of the entire room, directly against the south wall. Reaching toward it from the north wall was a second similar "cobble hearth," only slightly shorter than the first. And wedged into the corner opening between the ends of the two was a perfectly preserved metate bin set at an angle, its single Pueblo style grinding stone still in place but because of space limitation at a steeper slope than was customary for a Pueblo woman's grinding position.

One should have reached the east half of this crowded kitchen room only by stepping over the north-south "cobble hearth" just mentioned. The east division of this room (marked L) had two such hearths, separated by a few inches between their ends, against the east wall. A single metate bin filled the southeast corner of this room.

Adjoining apartment XIII on its south side was the remains of a room with no special features except what appeared to have been a wide doorway toward the corner of the south wall. Our guess was that this room had served as a dining area for the men who lived in those rooms just north of the "kitchen complex." Who? Possibly those who made up the religious unit of Onate's colonists? If so, this overall complex would have been the monastery.

By now, the first tones of fall were beginning to show in the changing colors of a leaf here, a leaf there, and we were pushing our trowel and shovel work so that we could have a few hours left for packing. No part of San Miguel del Yungue had yielded many artifacts during our three seasons, but several were of marked historic importance. We had found a fine museum quality 16th century bronze medal with the Trinity depicted in raised design on one side and a portrait of Saint Jerome with his beloved lion on the other apparently lost by a Spanish captain in one of the dark first floor inner storage rooms of the east mound area just north of the apartments we have described. There was a much corroded canon ball, various corroded chunks from brass and from iron chain armor, a wristlet from plate armor, embossed bronze buttons, a copper spoon (there was one on Onate's list), handles from copper vessels, a copper ring, a ferrule from a knife handle, some pieces apparently from arquebuses, a hawk bell, a gilt cord hair net, and a section of the gilt braid which decorated robes for the religious group. Distribution ranged from house fills and floors to the vicinity of the domed ovens and various layers of the old Pueblo-Spanish colonial ash pile.

In some of the apartments we surmised had belonged to the captains and the priests were found fragments of colored glass vessels from Spain and Africa, one the base of a stemmed wine glass but the others not identifiable as to original shape. In the floor sweepings of east mound rooms and also in the debris mound were scattered Venetian glass beads of assorted shapes and colors and bits of small Venetian mirrors, both brought for trade. Sherds of Mexican-made maiolica ware and even a few of delicate Chinese porcelain shipped to Mexico from the Orient obviously came from broken housewares of the elite.

But the artifact which most deighted us was an inlay decoration for a gun stock. A piece of animal bone (substituted for the ivory customarily used in Europe) had been used as the base on which the depiction of a walled Medieval city had been incised in a technique somewhat reminiscent of scrimshaw work. Behind the turreted city wall with its great entrance gate one could see the high terraced roofs of houses, their architectural style strongly suggesting that the carving had been made by the one young Flemish soldier whose name appears on the original census list of soldier-colonists accompanying Onate up from Mexico.

We were feeling farily well satisfied with what had been accomplished in the limited time of our three seasons. We had sampled the west mound sufficiently to have a basic understanding of it. The same was true for the northern portion of the east mound, and the central and southern portions of that east mound or house block had yielded the Spanish-modified apartments we had so hoped to uncover, plus examples of the earliest cooking platforms and also of the first domed ovens known for the United States.

We also had what certainly well might be the monastery, with its unique and crowded kitchen complex.

Nothing was lacking in our list or priorities except for that permanent church of San Miguel, which should have been near the monastery. But where?

And then! No more than 20 feet from the opening into the "kitchen complex" and its possible adjoining dining room, we did find that church!

We had been working westward, following the row of Spanish occupied apartments, of which there seemed to have been only one more between the "kitchen complex" and the east edge of Yungue's old central plaza. Going north from there, a few of the front apartments showed floor level doorways, but between those opening on the central plaza and those fronting one what we had been calling the "east plaza" was a block of first story rooms nine deep east-west and something more than nine deep north-south, very few of which had doorways, firepits, or other special features. In other words, this must have been, by original intent of the native builders, a first story block of storage rooms above which stood the living quarters of a large proportion of Yungue's original population and, later, of the first Spanish colonial population. In the fill of about half that block of rooms we had found corroded remnants of pieces of equipment so badly fragmentized that the original objects could not be named even by experts to whom we sent them for examination.

Other than in those rooms and in the ash pile out beyond the "east plaza," our major collection of this "metal trash" was coming from the dust of the "street" fronting what we were jocularly referring to as our "avenue of Spanish elite." (See Map of Distribution of Metal, Yungue, Summer 1962.) That "street" evidently had served as a thoroughfare between the barracks on the west mound and our area of concentration of the leaders of the colony along the south edge of the east house block.

But what was this we were running into in our final clearing of this street? Rocks? Ash and charcoal? And more rocks?

Yungue had been almost without rocks (stones) except for the cobbles used in the single-thickness foundations for the adobe walls. These were no cobbles!

Without question we were against a stone wall of poorly cut small blocks of volcanic tuff such as made up the Pajarito Plateau a few miles distant but could be found in minor deposits at much less distance. The stone wall was directly across the street (south side) from our line of modified coursed adobe apartments. When we found a corner to that stone wall, we collected all the students we could reasonably use, and set them to trowling along both wall surfaces, in both directions.

Within two days — there was no doubt — half of the long lost church of San Miguel had been outlined!

The north transept was clear, and in the adobe of its floor lay two male Indian burials within three feet of each other, one with a Spanish bronze or copper button with raised design which may have been worn on a cord as a decoration, and the other with a piece of bone marked with a cross lying on his chest. San Juan men who had served as sacristans?

The north wall of the nave extended eastward just at the fenceline that edged the little access road leading to the Martinez and Salazar houses. The little dirt road, in fact, ran right up the old nave of the church!

At the east end of the nave, the wall turned to the south, showing where the main doorway had opened to the sunrise. We already had found an opening midway in the north wall of the nave where a doorway had entered from the side.

Our overall measurement of 67 feet length for this church presupposed that there had been no protruding extension marking the center of the altar area, a point on which we, ourselves, had no evidence. Wall stubs still might be found outlining such a curve under the surface of that little road. The width of the nave (N-S) would have been between 25 and 30 feet; the width of the north transept (E-W) was 25 feet. (See Map of Church.)

How high the walls of volcanic tuff blocks had been we could not say; the greatest height of stone wall still existant was between 1½ and 2 feet. Originally the stone portion may have been appreciably higher and finished off with coursed adobe, or the church could have been built entirely of volcanic tuff blocks laid up in clay like the walls of many Pajarito Plateau Pueblos, with most of the stones from the church walls eventually disseminated by the bulldozer. Only one unidentifiable metal fragment and no sherds were found in the church, but two bronze candlesticks, not precisely matched but close enough to have been the pair which originally graced the church altar, were uncovered a few feet to the east of the structures we have discussed as the "kitchen complex" and dining room for the convent group.

How had this chapel met its destruction? We have no recorded details for the Spaniards had left, but one can guess. During the 1600s the original polite greeting of the Pueblos to the Spaniards had worn increasingly thin. In part this was the result of pressure by the church endeavoring to have the Indians completely forsake their old religion concentrating on the interaction of mankind and nature. Not until after the Pueblo rebellion did the priests permit something of a combination of the two religions, emphasizing their numerous parallels. The second major pressure resented by the Indians was Spanish insistence of a type of taxation involving work or contributions of food, woven goods, or other products — actually against Spanish law but carried out by those in power in this far isolated area.

When the overstrained Pueblos finally broke into a unified rebellion against the Spaniards in 1680, churches were burned and friars killed in a number of mission sites, as well as a major attack being made on Santa Fe itself and smaller attacks eliminating numerous ranch families. As Popé, the war chief of San Juan Pueblo, was one of the three main leaders of the rebellion, we can hardly suppose that the church of San Miguel at San Juan, the oldest symbol of what the Pueblos saw as one of the major threats against their old native culture did not have its roof burned and its walls thrown down during the initial thrusts of the revolutionists, even if no Spaniards then were living in San Gabriel del Yungue.

Adams and Chavez (1956:85:fn.2) mention that a new church is known to have been under construction in San Juan Pueblo shortly after 1706, so we can surmise that little if anything remained of the original structure by that date. The period of use of the disintegrating mounds of San Gabriel del Yungue for burials presumably would have dated from 1610, when Peralta saw to the move of the remaining colonists to Santa Fe, and years after 1706, when the new church had ceased to be a novelty and its yard became acceptable as a cemetery.

By the end of August, 1962, San Gabriel del Yungue, the first Spanish settlement and capital in our Southwest, and its San Miguel Church once more were securely located and their portraits sketched in. In reality, all that remains of this site definitely should be excavated to sterile base soil and the remains of walls, even if only a few inches high, preserved. Soil removed should be sifted through one-quarter inch or finer screen so that even the tiniest remains such as the Venetian glass beads would be retrieved. Yungue's north and south mounds, if they ever existed, definitely need investigation; their house blocks or the spaces left without Indian or Spanish construction should be mapped like the east and west mounds. The south wall bases of the church must be uncovered and preserved — and the walls we traced within the edge of the roadway should be re-excavated and preserved — and the interfering access road over which unaware drivers daily run their cars up the nave where worshippers knelt almost four centuries ago *must be relocated.* There is only one "oldest church of which remains still exist" in the United States.

History, which documents the growth of mankind, can be understood only through what it leaves in contemporary writing and in the material creations and possessions of the persons who were responsible for a specific episode. The past is the heritage of us all, its problems, its successes, its story of human beings with different cultural backgrounds endeavoring, struggling, to work out problems based on human needs and a combination of the exigencies of nature and their times.

What one man may cast away for personal gain can be a loss to all of humanity forever.

# BIBLIOGRAPHY

Adams, Eleanor B. and Fray Angelico Chavez. 1956. *The Missions of New Mexico, 1776,* A Description by Fray Atonasio Dominguez. Translation and annotation. UNM Press, Albuquerque.

Bandelier, Adolph F.A. 1890. Final Report of Investigation Amoung the Indians of the Southwestern United States, Carried on Mainly in the Years from 1880 to 1885. Vol. I. *Papers of the Archeological Institute of America,* American Series 3. Cambridge, Mass.

_____. 1892. Final Report of Investigation Amoung the Indians of the Southwestern United States, Carried on Mainly in the Years from 1880 to 1885. Vol. II. *Papers of the Archaeological Institute of America,* American Series 4. Cambridge, Mass.

Bolton, Herbert E. 1930. *Spanish Expeditions in the Southwest.* New York.

Boyd, E. 1943. Antiques in New Mexico. *The Magazine Antiques,* Vol XVIV:2: 58-62. New York

_____. 1961. Bronze Medal of Sixteenth Century Style. *El Palacio* 68:2:124-128.

Breternitz, David A. 1966. An Appraisal of Tree-Ring Dated Pottery in the Southwest. *Anthropological Papers of the University of Arizona 10.* Tucson.

Dozier, Edward P. 1970. *The Pueblo Indians of North America, Case Studies in Cultural Anthropology.* Eds. G. and L. Spindler. Stanford.

Ellis, Florence Hawley. 1970d. Irrigation and Water Works in the Rio Grande. Ms. Paper given at the Pecos Conference Symposium, Santa Fe, New Mexico.

_____. 1970e. San Gabriel del Yunque: Window on the Prespanish Indian World. Ms. 20 pgs.

Forrest, Earle R. 1929. *Missions and Pueblos of the Old Southwest.* Their Myths, Legends, Fiestas and Ceremonies, with some accounts of the Indian tribes and their dances and of the Penitentes. Arthur H. Clark Co., Cleveland, U.S.A. (Reprinted by Rio Grande Press, Chicago, 1965).

Fink, Colin G. and E.P. Polushkin. 1946. Metallographic Examination of the San Gabriel Bell Fragment. *New Mexico Historical Review.* XXI;2:145-148. Santa Fe.

Harris, Arthur H. 1969. The Mammalion Remains from Yungue. Ms. 39 pgs. Museum of Arid Land Biology. The University of Texas at El Paso.

Hammond, George P. 1940. *Narratives of the Coronado Expedition.* UNM Press. Albuquerque.

_____ and Agapito Rey. 1953. *Don Juan de Onate: Colonizer of New Mexico, 1595-1628.* Coronado Quarto Centenial Publication, Vol. I and II. UNM Press. Albuquerque.

Lambert, Marjorie F. 1952. Oldest Armor in the U.S. Discovered at San Gabriel del Yungue. *El Palacio* 59:3:83-87. (Description of the find by Jose Abeyta and note of Marge's work and on find of "piece of bronze bell" by Stephen Trujillo.)

_____. 1953. The Oldest Armor found in the United States. The San Gabriel del Yunque Helmet. *Archaeology* 6:2:108-110.

Mera, Harry P. 1935. Ceramic Clues to the Prehistory of North Central New Mexico. *New Mexico Archaeological Survey, Laboratory of Anthropology Technical Series Bulletin 8*. Santa Fe.

Peterson, Harold L. 1952. The Helmet Found at San Gabriel del Yungue, New Mexico. *El Palacio* 59:9:283-287 (Identification plus data on methods used for its preservation by Peterson.)

Scholes, France V. 1937. Church and State in New Mexico, 1610-1650. *Historical Society of New Mexico Publications in History*, Vol. VII. Albuquerque.

Smiley, Terah L., Stanley A. Stubbs, and Byrant Bannister. 1953. A foundation for the Dating of Some Late Archaeological Sites in the Rio Grande Area, New Mexico: Based on Studies in Tree-Ring Methods and Pottery Analysis. *Laboratory of Tree-Ring Research Bulletin No. 6*. University of Arizona Bulletin. Tucson.

Stowe, Noel R. 1982. *A Preliminary Report on the Pine Log Creek Site Ba462*. Ms. University of South Alabama Archaeological Research Laboratory, Mobile, Alabama.

Stubbs, Stanley A. and W.S. Stallings, Jr. 1953. The Excavation of Pindi Pueblo, New Mexico. *Monographs of the School of American Research 18*. Santa Fe.

Tichy, Marjorie F. 1944. Exploratory Work at Yuque Yunque. *El Palacio* LI:11:222-224.

_____. 1946. New Mexico's First Capital. *New Mexico Historical Review*. XXI:2:140-144.

_____. 1946. First Capital Suffers Further Damage. *El Palacio*. 53:11:324.

Villagra, Gaspar Perez de. 1933. *A History of New Mexico by Gaspar Perez de Villagra*. Alcala 1610. Translated from the Spanish by Gilbert Espenosa, Ed. Introduction and notes by F.W. Hodge. *The Los Angeles Quivera Society, Vol IV*. Los Angeles.

# THE SPANIARDS OF SAN GABRIEL
## Marc Simmons

When New Mexico's first governor, the *adelantado* Don Juan de Onate, arrived on the upper Rio Grande in 1598, he selected the Espanola Valley as the site for a settlement and his capital.* That district was inhabited by the Tewa Pueblos who were known to be more hospitable toward the Spaniards than were people farther down river. For example, the Tiwas living in the neighborhood of modern Bernalillo were barely able to conceal their hostility when the Onate expedition passed by. They had not forgotten the ill-treatment suffered at the hands of Francisco Vasquez de Coronado in the years 1540-1542.

Until the appearance of Governor Onate, the people of San Juan Pueblo had experienced only passing contact with Europeans. So, when the Spaniards decided to settle at their pueblo, they accepted the newcomers with some grace. A year or so later, Onate is believed to have moved his people across the Rio Grande to San Gabriel del Yunge Oweenge. The transfer, no doubt, was an expression of the Spaniards' desire to have their own community, but it may have been prompted as much by growing tension with the San Juans who probably felt their guests had overstayed their welcome.

The behavior of the Spaniards toward the Pueblo people in general and the San Juans in particular was conditioned by their history, culture, and national psychology as well as by certain local deficiencies in the environment which produced their own set of stresses. A review of Spanish character and motives at the time of the occupation of New Mexico will help us to understand better the beginnings of the little San Gabriel settlement.

The Onate colonists, like their countrymen everywhere, felt a strong sense of pride in being Spanish. Spain at the end of the sixteenth century was at its peak, its worldwide empire stretching to

---

*Some question has been raised recently over whether San Juan/San Gabriel was actually the capital of New Mexico. The matter is easily settled. Since this place was the seat and residence of the governor and the only settlement in the kingdom, it automatically became the capital. In a letter of May 30, 1599, Onate referred to it as the capital, and, he was in the best position to know. Further, Dr. George P. Hammond, Onate's biographer, regarded it as the capital, so that would seem to end the discussion.*

far-flung points of the compass. Conquest and colonization had become a patriotic duty. In expanding the boundaries of the realm, the individual Spaniard could feel a sense of personal involvement in the making of history and the carrying out of royal policy. His pioneering on the frontier, therefore, seemed to him a noble mission since it advanced the cause of the nation.

But more, of course, than simple patriotism led those first recruits to join Juan de Onate's colonizing expedition. They were animated also by a strong thirst for adventure, by the chance to exchange a humdrum life at home for the excitement of finding and exploring new lands. The lure of adventuring was a mighty attraction for the Spaniard, as Cervantes demonstrated so forcefully in his tale of Don Quixote. As that story illustrates, however, the road to adventure can be filled with peril and disappointment, a fact the first New Mexicans discovered to their sorrow.

As an outlet for their surplus energies, Spanish men of the sixteenth century commonly joined military enterprises. Those following Onate were practically all described as soldiers, although many possessed other skills and occupations, such as those of miner, farrier, and barber. Owing to the distinctive course of Iberian history, the profession of arms was one of the most prestigious in Spanish society, and youths by the thousands flocked to the military banner.

For eight centuries, beginning in A.D. 711, Spaniards had fought the Moors in the old country. The Moors were invaders out of Africa and non-Christians, members of the Moslem religion. The long holy crusade waged against them firmly implanted the militaristic spirit in Spain and also helped to bring the soldier and the priest together as allies in a common cause. The ultimate victory over the Moors gave the Spaniards a towering confidence in themselves and led to the conviction that both their wars and their religion had the support of the Almighty. This conceit was reinforced by early Spanish successes in the New World.

The first Spaniards on the Rio Grande drew a parallel between their own experiences here and the crusading efforts of their grandfathers in Spain. Were they not campaigning to spread Christianity and extend the domain of the King just as their forebearers had done in the long struggle with the Moors? As if to bear that out, the first New Mexican chroniclers frequently alluded to the apparent similarity between Southwest tribes and the Moslem people. Some of the Plains Indians, they noted, used bows like the Moors and painted (tattooed?) their chins in the fashion of Moorish

40

women. And they observed that the Pueblos worshipped in underground chambers which Spanish writers initially called mosques (religious temples of the Moors) meaning, of course, the ceremonial kivas.

We can recall, as well, that soon after Onate reached San Juan his people staged the old open-air folk drama, *Los moros y cristianos*, which is still performed in New Mexico today. The play, enacted on horseback and including a lively battle between Christians and Moors, depicted the triumph of Spanish arms and religion. Likely its performance on this first occasion was intended to symbolize the new Spanish dominance over New Mexico and its native people. In any case, it is quite clear that the experience with the Moors was still fresh in the minds of the Onate colonists. With the weight of history guiding their thinking, they tended to look upon themselves as latter-day crusaders and that attitude colored and shaped their relations with the Pueblo people.

The religious motive was also behind the Spanish advance into New Mexico. Spread of Hispanic Catholicism was a primary objective of the royal government which provided both funding and direction for the missionary program. Under that system there existed no boundary between religion and everyday life as is the case in modern society. In this, the Spaniard's view coincided with that of the Pueblo who believed that religious practice formed the framework uniting all spheres of human endeavor. But the two differed markedly in matters of approach and tolerance. While Pueblos took a liberal stance in extending respect to differing religious customs, the Spaniards proved unwilling to countenance anything but wholesale submission to their own state-run Catholicism. Their inflexibility in that regard would lead eventually to monumental disaster for New Mexico.

The religious motive was of considerable practical importance to Governor Onate because it led the government to furnish him six Fransciscan priests and two lay brothers and pay all their expenses in the New Mexican venture. In many letters to the Viceroy and King, Onate speaks as if his main reason for settling on the Rio Grande was to convert the Pueblo Indians. And indeed, under Spanish law at this time, subjugation of Native Americans could only be carried out beneath the guise of extending to them the fruits of the Christian religion.

In this attitude and in this emphasis upon the significance of the proposed missionary program, Juan de Onate was engaging in a good deal of pretending. He was saying in his letters what he knew his superiors wanted to hear. In truth, his strongest motive and greatest interest in New Mexico lay in another direction.

The principal reason both Onate and his soldiers undertook this colonization effort on a far frontier was that they expected to get rich. They hoped to achieve that by finding lodes of silver or other precious metals. Actually their expectations were founded on something more than the will-of-the-wisp dreams of treasure-laden Indian kingdoms that had beguiled Coronado more than a half century before.

From reports of previous exploratory expeditions, Onate was aware that the landscape of New Mexico with its isolated mountain ranges and mesas separated by semi-arid expanses of flatland bore a strong resemblance to the physical geography of northern Mexico where silver had already been discovered in abundance. The mountains of Zacatecas, Nueva Vizcaya (modern Durango and Chihuahua), Coahuila, and Nuevo Leon were humming with the activity of prosperous mining camps. Hence, it was not unreasonable to anticipate that New Mexico, upon being fully explored, would yield similar wealth to those Spaniards intrepid enough to get in on the ground floor.

That prospect helps explain why many of Onate's companions were willing to sell or mortgage valuable properties in Mexico to raise the funds that would allow them to participate in the opening of New Mexico. By expending their personal fortunes, they hoped to reap a larger financial reward in the future, thereby improving not only their economic position but their social status as well.

The same aim, on a grander scale, animated Juan de Onate. By gaining the right under a royal grant to invade and organize the land of the Pueblos into a new Spanish kingdom, he immediately enhanced his place in history. But his reputation, as he well understood, depended upon his ability to carry the project through to a successful conclusion. Therefore, he unstintingly threw all of his energies and all of the family fortune, accumulated by his father in the Zacatecas silver strike, into the New Mexican effort. In total, he may have risked something like the equivalent of a million dollars.

At the beginning, the outlook was exceedingly bright. Onate brought with him dedication and a capacity for leadership. By background he was well-versed in the methods of discovering, mining, and smelting silver. And he came ably provisioned with the tools and equipment required in the development of a mining economy.

The governor's personal tragedy was that during his nine-year tenure, he failed to make a silver strike. That was in spite of a diligent search in which he led prospecting expeditions outward in all directions from San Gabriel. Ranging northward into the Rockies of Colorado, eastward to the plains of Kansas, and westward as far as the Gulf of California, he collected promising mineral samples on every hand to take back for assaying. But none proved rich enough to merit full-scale mining. Interestingly, some of those samples were recovered by archeologists when San Gabriel was excavated during several seasons in the early 1960s.

The failure to make a major find explains why Onate gradually lost the loyalty of a portion of his men, some of whom even mutinied and deserted. In the end, the colony, as Onate had planned it, fell apart simply because no ready source of wealth could be found to support it. When that became evident, the remaining Spaniards imposed an increasing burden on the Pueblos whose tight economies were ill-prepared to sustain the needs of outsiders. That pattern, established by the first settlers at San Gabriel, persisted well into the century and contributed to the outbreak of the Pueblo Revolt in 1680.

Onate and his men in their initial optimism had intended to create a new and brilliant center of Hispanic civilization on the upper Rio Grande. In their supply train of wagons and carts, they carried seeds and cuttings, tools, domestic implements, religious articles and even elegant clothing of the kind they were accustomed to wear at fancy dress balls and festivals. In their traveling trunks, men had packed velvet suits with lace cuffs and fluted collars and shoes of fine-tooled Cordovan leather. Women had brought silk dresses, embroidered mantillas, tortoise shell combs, and richly decorated dancing slippers. All these things they planned to use in the mansions and palaces they meant to build with the profits from their new-found silver mines. But the poverty of New Mexico and the harsh realities of the frontier soon made clear that such clothes had little place in this isolated Spanish province. Within a generation, New Mexicans were dressing in rough attire made of buckskin and coarse cloth, in a style similar to that of the Pueblo Indians, one conforming to the realities of local life.

One of the great ironies of our regional history lies in the fact that Onate and every Spaniard who came after him failed to make a major find of silver or gold anywhere in the Southwest. The stars must have been arrayed against them, for the mineral was there. But all of it would await discovery by Anglo American prospectors in the nineteenth century — the Colorado gold at Cripple Creek and in the San Juan Mountains; the fabulous Comstock silver lode of Nevada; California's placer gold; the rich deposits of Arizona; and New Mexico's own treasure horde in the Sangre de Cristo and Ortiz Mountains of the north and the Black Range and Mogollon Mountains of the south. The Spaniards, through no lack of trying on their part, missed it all.

Had luck been better and led them to stumble upon any one of those bonanzas, we can imagine that the ensuing mining boom would have produced a rush of population from the south and led to the growth of a large and flourishing Spanish center, of the kind dreamed of by Onate. Had that occurred, the subsequent history of the Far West would certainly have evolved in a different way. That such a development failed to overtake New Mexico, while a misfortune for Spanish interests, must be judged a decided blessing for the Pueblo Indians. The added stresses and pressures piled upon them by a much greater Hispanic population might well have smothered native culture and extinguished tribal units.

By late 1609, with Juan de Onate having departed New Mexico under a cloud, a new governor, Don Pedro de Peralta, oversaw the transfer of the capital from San Gabriel to a new site at Santa Fe. It has generally been assumed that San Gabriel was abandoned at that time. But reference to the place can be found in the documents as late as 1617. So it is apparent that the little community struggled on for a number of years before it finally withered away.

A study of the Onate years at San Juan and San Gabriel allows us to enlarge our understanding of the processes that occur when two cultures meet and experience conflict and eventual accommodation. While yawning gaps exist in the story, enough information is available to define the general picture and draw useful conclusions. And the Onate episode also can remind us that although we cannot tamper with history and change what was done in the past, we *can* learn something valuable from the lessons of human experience.

44

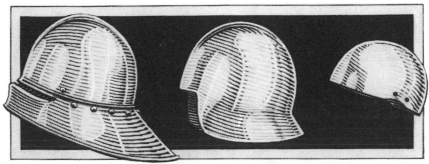

*These artist's renditions illustrate some of the possible ways the archer's helmet may have looked. Illustrations by Glen Strock.*

*Spanish military helmet found at Yungue;*
*Top: Side View, Bottom: Back View;*
*Courtesy of Museum of NM, Neg. Nos. 46664 & 46665*

*Aerial view of entire Yungue site*

*View of end of trenches*

*View of Spanish area of Yungue, footings*

*Uncle Steve with a pot*

*Panorama of Yungue site*

*Corner of Church foundation*

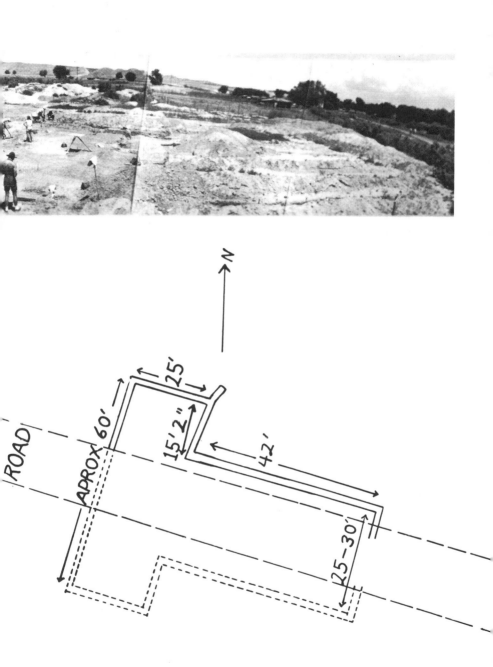

ROAD

N

25'

APROX 60'

15' 2"

42'

25 — 30'

*The San Miguel Church at San Gabriel del Yungue*

NOTE:
1. All Walls are of stone
based contruction except
where noted.
2. Heavy lines and roman
numerals indicate size and
number of Apartments.
3. Capital letters indicate
separate rooms and areas.

LEGEND
ⓜ Micaceous Bowl
◖ Post Hole
● Firepit
▯ Metate
⊡ Stone Table
Ⴑ Metate Bin
x Indian Burial

Scale 1" = approx. 19'

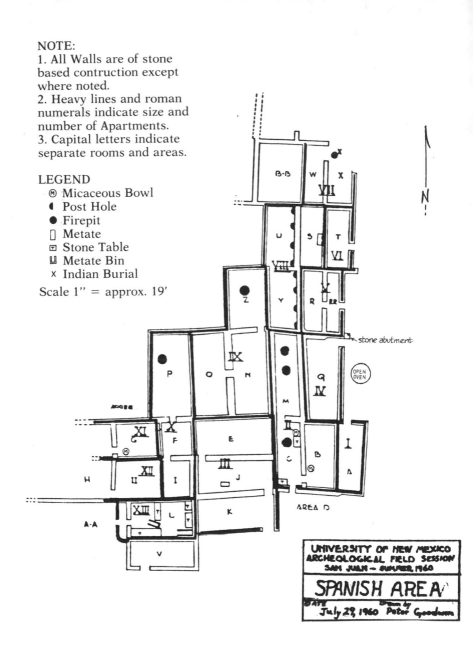

*Plan of Yungue Spanish Area*

52

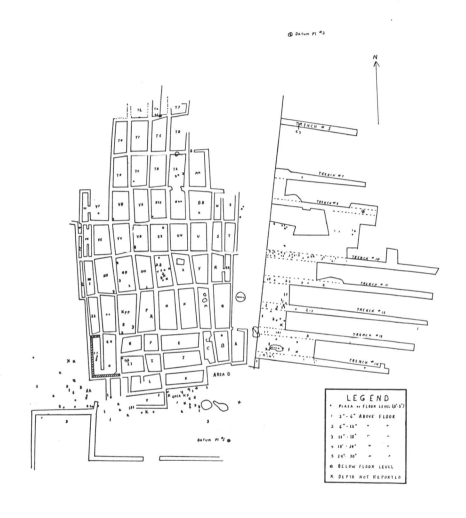

*Distribution of Metal at Yungue — Summer, 1962*

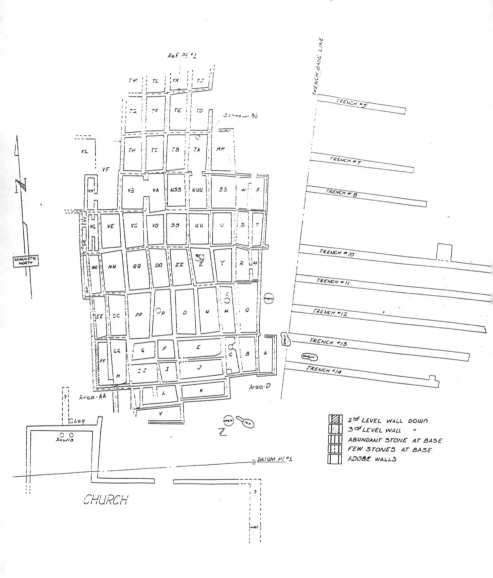

*BSJ Yungue East mound — Spanish*

*Dr. F.H. Ellis (pointing) directing her crew in working on the Church area*

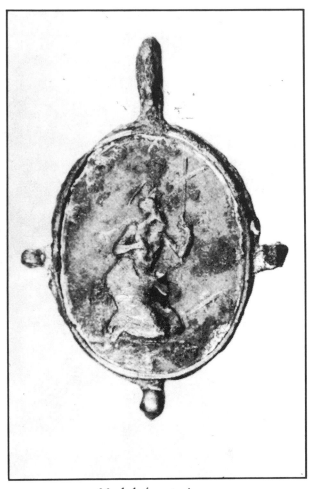

*Medal, front view*
*7/8 inch length, 5/8 inch width*

*Medal, back view*

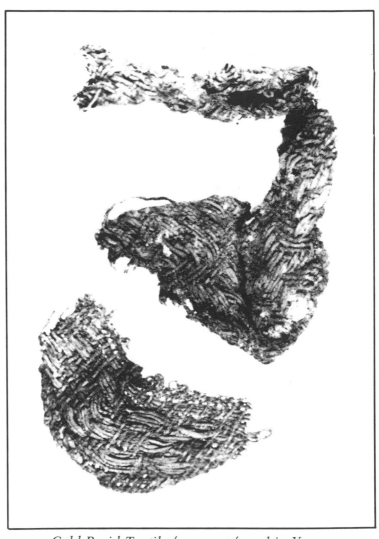

*Gold Braid Textile fragment found in Yungue*

*Links of Chain Mail found in Yungue*

*Candlestick base*

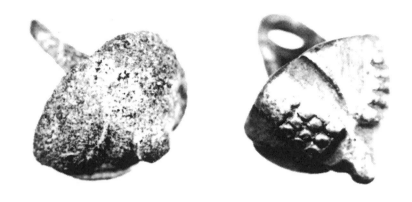

*Brass Buttons found in Yungue*

*Some Spanish objects found at Yungue*

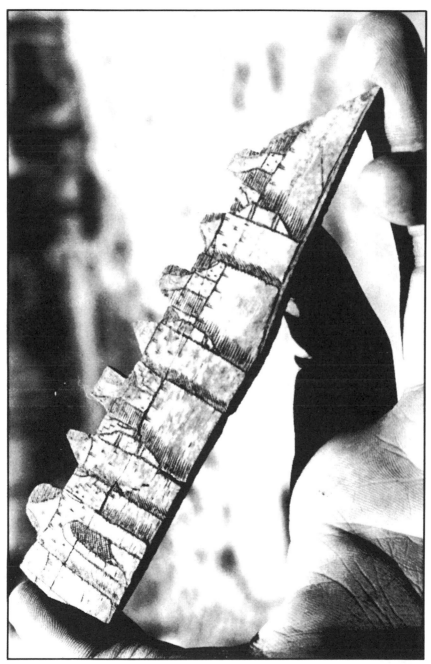

*Engraved Gunstock inset in hand*

*Three whole Indian vessels dug up at Yungue*

# ONATE'S ADMINISTRATION AND THE PUEBLO INDIANS

*Myra Ellen Jenkins*

The summer of 1598 was a momentous one in the history of New Mexico, especially for the original inhabitants whose land was being invaded, and particularly for the Pueblo of San Juan. On July 10, Juan de Onate, bearing the titles of governor and captain general, led an advance party of his colonizing expedition composed of officers, scouts and two Franciscan friars into the Pueblo which he called *Ohke*, then promptly renamed "San Juan Bautista," later called "San Juan de los Caballeros."[1] After stopping at many pueblos along the way he established this village as headquarters for the permanent settlement of the northern frontier. On August 18, he was joined by the main body of his 129-soldier colonists, many with their families, and eight additional Franciscans who had been proceeding at a slower rate up the Rio Grande valley, and then by way of the Galisteo through the Pueblo of San Marcos to avoid the rugged mountains. The expedition had often been in straits for food in spite of the largesse of some of the pueblos through which they had come. One of them, a Piro pueblo on the opposite side of the river from which the caravan had halted on June 14, they called "Socorro" (Help) "because it furnished us with much maize."[2]

There is some question as to where these colonists initially settled. Most secondary accounts say it was at San Juan Pueblo proper but that the settlement was moved to the west side of the Rio Grande into the Pueblo of Yunque, renamed San Gabriel, some time during the next few months.[3] There is no mention of such a move having been made in the documents, however. I submit that the colonists were probably settled at San Gabriel from the beginning, although throughout 1599 Onate signed documents at San Juan Bautista, which he apparently designated as his personal headquarters. My basis for San Gabriel as the single settlement comes from two accounts, written in 1601 during an investigation of Onate's regime. In a letter to the viceroy dated from San Gabriel, March 22, 1601 Luis de Velasco stated that the expedition had been at the place from which he was writing for three years.[4] In July a Gines de Herrera Horta also stated that Onate had established the colonists at San Gabriel in the houses of the Indians, but for which Spanish doors and windows were fashioned.[5]

Don Juan de Onate was a person of no mean status. The son of the discoverer of the rich Zacetecas mines and founder of the city of the same name, Cristobal de Onate, and of aristocratic Dona Catalina de Salazar and married to the granddaughter of both Cortes and the Aztec ruler Moctezuma, he had signed a lengthy contract with Viceroy Luis de Velasco in 1595 authorizing him to undertake the colonization of New Mexico, largely at his own expense, for which his family put up much of the funding. But Velasco was reassigned and the new viceroy, the Count of Monterrey, was not sympathetic and three long years dragged by until the contract was finally ratified by the Crown. Finally, in April, 1598 the expedition set forth — a long caravan equipped with everything, it was hoped, the new colony would need to get started — all kinds of livestock, plants and seeds, tools, iron, nails, horseshoes, armaments, medicines, etc. One item which has always intrigued me in the lengthy inventory is 828 pairs of shoes and boots on the governor's list alone (if I have counted correctly). On April 20 the lumbering retinue reached the Rio Grande below El Paso and ten days later, on Ascension Day, Onate proclaimed the official occupation of "todos los reynos y provincias de Nuevo Mejico" in the name of Felipe II. The expedition crossed the river which they aptly called "El Rio del Norte," on May 4.[6]

According to the contract, this was a settlement expedition, not for conquest. The day of the arrogant conquistador who had taken what he wanted in a quest for mineral wealth and glory was now legally over. A reform wave had swept the Spanish colonial world since Francisco Vasquez de Coronado had clanked through the region more than 50 years before, seizing supplies from the pueblos regardless of their needs and treating the inhabitants as he wished. Due in large part to a crusading Dominican, Fray Bartolome de las Casas, who had gained the attention of the king and pricked the royal conscience. As a result, the colonial institutions of the empire had been reformed and specifically described in the many cedulas and ordinances issued by the Crown through the Council of the Indies. The intent was to protect the personal rights of the Indians as well as to safeguard their communal land and water rights. By the time of the *entrada* Indians had the legal position of being both royal vassals and also wards of the Crown.[7] Let us turn briefly to these institutions which Onate brought with him to New Mexico.

By all odds the worst institution of 16th century colonial administration, and the most misunderstood to this day, was that of the *encomienda*. A labor grant in the beginnng, the encomienda *was never a land grant*. Its piously stated purpose was the "commending" of Indian communities to the patronage of a Spaniard who was to provide for their Christianization and protection (protection from whom?). In return, the encomendero had the right to demand labor and tribute of goods and/or foodstuffs. The result had been virtual enslavement. But the "New Laws" of Charles V in 1541-1543 attempted to curb and eventually to eliminate the system, one provision stating "The Indians are free persons and vassals of the Crown."[8] In 1549 the Indians were freed of labor and their obligations limited to tribute only — and encomenderos were forbidden to even live on the lands of the Indians they held in encomienda.[9] Unfortunately, Spaniards were still given the right of the *repartimiento*, alltoments of Indians for brief periods of labor in agriculture, mines, etc. but for wages so that in theory *paid forced labor* replaced forced labor.[10]

During this period laws and regulations had also been issued to protect Indian land and water rights. Most of these were for the benefit of long-settled village communities in southern Mexico — belatedly to protect them from encroachment — communities with which the New Mexico pueblos had much in common. The basic decree was one of 1533: "They [the governors and viceroys] shall leave to the Indians their lands, patrimony and pastures in such a way that the Indians may not lack what they need and that they may have all the relief and repose possible for the support of their homes and families."[11] Other laws granted the original inhabitants additional grants if they needed more land, and forbade grants to be made to Spaniards, especially for grazing (*estancias*), near enough to Indian lands to cause damage.[12] As colonization spread north of the Valley of Mexico, the policy became one of gathering up nomadic groups, as most of the native peoples were not living in permanent village communities, and placing them on lands suitable for cultivation known as *reducciones*, somewhat similar to the U.S. Indian reservation system. A 1573 cedula specified land rights for these Indians in that such sites "shall have advantages of water, land and wood, entrances and exits and lands for cultivation, and an exido [common land] of a league in length where the Indians can have their stock without their mixing with those of the Spaniards."[13] The reduccion was, however, under the supposed "protection" of a nearby Spaniard and was most often attempted in areas of mineral developments. Unfortunately the system made it easy to allot the Indians on reducciones for encomienda tribute and labor in mines.

Closely allied to the civil reduccion was the religious *congregation* — the gathering up of wandering natives and placing them under the tutelage of friars from one of the missionary orders in areas where there were no resources to exploit. The friars were to persuade the Indians to settle down and to lay out the mission community in the standard town pattern with the church located in the center and the dwellings in blocks around the plaza. They were to teach the natives how to construct acequias and to raise crops. After ten years the lands were to be turned over to the Indians as their own property. [14]

These were the colonial institutions with all the protective measures which were included in the far-reaching *Ordinances of His Majesty for the New Discoveries, Conquests and Pacifications* issued by Felipe II in 1573 to be followed in the settlement of new areas such as New Mexico. Only authorized leaders who signed contracts incorporating its terms could take settlement expeditions into new lands. Specific patterns were laid down for the founding of Spanish towns and settlements and establishing procedures for local government. Throughout, it was mandated that the Indians were vassals and were to be treated with consideration and moderation. [15] Onate's contract, specified that he had no right which violated the 1573 Ordinances which he promised to follow:

> Both during the organization and progress of the expedition and
> after the people have been reduced and placed under obedience to
> the royal crown, you must observe all that is contained in the royal
> order issued at Bosque de Segovia on July 13, 1573 containing the
> royal ordinances for new discoveries in the Indies, as well as the
> contract made with you by virtue of those ordinances for the ex-
> pedition . . . [16]

The phrase "placed under obedience to the royal crown" referred to the oaths of vassalage to the Crown which the Indians were to take. Before arriving at San Juan, Onate had administered this oath at Santo Domingo Pueblo on July 7 to leaders of seven Indian groups. On September 9 at San Juan Bautista he assembled a number of Indian leaders, "in the main kiva of this pueblo," in addition to those of San Juan, and after a harangue about the blessings of occupations and the virtues and attributes of King Felipe, administered to them the feudal oaths of allegiance, thereby making them in reality royal vassals. They knelt and promised, through their interpreters, to obey the king, their lord, in all things. Obviously, the leaders had little comprehension that this colorful ceremony meant giving up of much of their own independence.[17]

One of the rights which Onate had requested, but which he had been denied, was his right to determine the amount of encomienda tribute or the tribute paid to the governor. However, he was permitted to allot encomienda for tribute purposes and collect for the Crown in moderation and subject to approval of the Viceroy. Royal tributes were collected and as time went on became one of the worst abuses of his and other administrations. Encomienda allotments were not made for several years, and the number of encomenderos was finally fixed at 32.[18] In 1602 the Council of the Indies established encomienda as either a manta or a hide and a *fanega* of corn (1½ bushels) per year for each household.[19] Unhappily, there is much evidence that more was illegally frequently demanded.

It was expected that the reduccion system would be applied in New Mexico, but the Spaniards found the pueblos already living in fixed abodes and hence they were entitled to the full protection of the land laws for settled villages. In fact, all of the institutions were modified by actual conditions. The New Mexican from the beginning, whether Indian or non-Indian, has always had a history of refusing to fit precisely into any pattern. The Franciscan Order was entrusted with conversion, but the Ordinances had enjoined them from using methods other than patience and persuasion:

> *In order to do this they will not begin by rebuking them for their vices and idolatries or by taking from them their women or their idols so that they are offended or become hostile to Christian doctrine. Rather they must first be taught and after they are instructed they will be persuaded of their own free will to abandon that which is contrary to our Holy, Catholic Faith and evangelical doctrine.*[20]

The Franciscans who came with Onate assumed that they would establish congregaciones but that system would not work, for the Pueblo Indians were already living in settled agricultural communities. San Juan Indians and others could indeed teach the padres a thing or two about constructing acequias and raising crops with little water, since they had been doing so for generations. All pueblos had their own tribal government. The Onate record states that the Colonizer began the construction of the church at San Juan on August 23, and that it was actually completed on September 7. (This was obviously a temporary structure, probably of jacal construction, since Dr. Ellis' investigation revealed a much more pretentious one built at San Gabriel.) After

67

dedicating the structure on September 9 and receiving the oaths of allegiance, Onate assigned the friars to groups of pueblos. Father Cristobal de Salazar was to minister to the Tewas, including San Juan and San Gabriel. The pueblos were *not* assigned to the friars — an important difference. The mission churches and conventos were built at one side of the plaza, or at least off center, so that the pueblos kept the native religious orientation of the kiva as well as that of the new Catholic faith. The friars were allotted plots within Indian fields tilled for them, but the land belonged to the natives, and was not the friars to develop or assign.[21]

It would appear that Onate in the beginning fulfilled the terms of the contract with respect to the rights of those whose lands he had invaded in a peaceful occupation. But his real mission was to permanently settle colonists, to discover and explore new areas, to find a route to the Southern Sea, to find mineral wealth if any existed, and all this for the benefit of the empire and the Europeans, not for the benefit of the original inhabitants who were still a subject people in spite of all protective measures. Problems soon arose, and in the process of confronting them events occurred which illustrated just how tenuous such protective measures really were. There is little question that Onate from the beginning intended to abide by the terms of his bargain, but he could not control many of his soldiers and when "push came to shove," in modern vernacular, he over-reacted and then attempted to justify his actions to his superiors in a maze of legal manipulations.

The first major confrontation took place late in 1598. In October, Onate was exploring the Saline Piro pueblos east of the Manzano Mountain, then decided to attempt to find a route to the Southern Sea, and headed west, visiting Acoma high on its penol where he was welcomed by the people and given supplies, thence to Zuni and the Hopis. Captain Marcos Farfan headed north to investigate stories of mines, then back to Zuni where Onate's nephew the Maese de Campo Juan de Zaldivar was to meet Onate with additional forces for the South Sea trip as soon as his brother Vicente de Zaldivar returned from an expedition into the eastern plains. Juan stopped at Acoma on December 4 and disaster struck. The accounts vary as to what happened. Zaldivar and a portion of the forces climbed the great rock, leaving some 18 soldiers to guard the horses at the base. The Acomas attacked, killing Zaldivar and 12 others; a few escaped by jumping off the cliff. Onate in the meantime had decided to return to San Juan and on the way from Zuni was met by the survivors with the sad tale. The colonizer forthwith returned to San Juan and prepared for a strong punitive expedition since his authority as the representative of Imperial Spain could not permit such open defiance by a pueblo whose leaders had taken the oath of allegiance, and then killed nearly one-tenth of his army. In good bureaucratic fashion he assembled his officers and the padres for a *junta de guerra* which declared that a campaign against the rebel Acomas was a "just war." Vicente de Zaldivar, boiling with vengeance over the death of his brother, was placed in charge. After two days of vicious fighting, the pueblo was captured. One account says that some of those who first surrendered were placed in a kiva, then taken out one by one, stabbed and thrown over the cliff, and the Indians still bitterly resisted, entrenching themselves in kivas and underground passages which Zaldivar ordered set afire. Those finally taken prisoner and the women and children were hauled off to Santo Domingo on February 9, 1599 and there the lengthy trial of the leaders was conducted. According to Onate's account, the evidence showed that the Zaldivar group had gone to the pueblo in peace to secure supplies and had been treacherously beset upon.[22] According to others, Spaniards all, testifying before the Valverde investigation of Onate in 1601 and again before his *residencia*, the detachment secured some supplies, started for Zuni, and then turned back and seized more, at which action the Acomas resisted. This version sounds much more plausible, since Onate only a few days before had been welcomed and provisioned. Spaniards also testified as to Zaldivar's treachery in taking the first captives under peace negotiations and then murdering them.[23] After lengthy proceedings Onate delivered his sentence. Men over 25 were to have one foot cut off and placed in servitude to a Spaniard for 20 years. This type of enslavement was legal in the case of a "just war." Males between 12 and 25 were also given 20 years, but no mutilation, as were all women over 12 years. Younger children were placed under the supervision of Spanish officials; a couple of Hopis who had taken part in the fray were condemned to the loss of their right arms and sent to their people as examples.[24] There is some evidence, however, that these terms as dictated and sent to the viceroy were intended to prove how constant Onate was in dealing with those who had gone astray from their vows of allegiance, but that they were exaggerated. Witnesses later testified that there had been some amputation, but that most of the captives had escaped and no measures had been taken to stop them from reestablishing their pueblo.[25] At any rate, within a few years Acoma was again a strong pueblo, which would have been impossible had all the adults been placed in servitude.

During 1599 another punitive expedition, not quite as severe, was also launched against the Jumano Pueblo, located at present Gran Guivira monument, for which Onate was also later held to account.[26] Charges of seizure of supplies and illegal tribute and Indian labor were also levelled. In 1607 Onate resigned and returned to Mexico, only to face years of official investigation for his conduct in the residencia of his administration. When matters came to the actual trial in 1614 he was found guilty of twelve charges, one of which involved the hanging of two Acomas and another the undue severity of his sentences after the revolt was crushed. For these and offenses also against Spaniards he was condemned to perpetual exile from New Mexico, banishment from Mexico City itself for four years, loss of his titles and a whopping fine. Some of his lieutenants did not go unscathed either, and were also found guilty of crimes against Acoma, including Vicente de Zaldivar.[27]

The interesting thing about the whole affair is that some Spaniards felt strongly enough about failure to abide by colonial legal processes to testify against a person with the status of Onate. As the 17th century wore along (and wore along is correct), other governors were even more lax in enforcing the ordinances and regulations, and the Franciscans also all too often forgot their instructions to convert with patience and gentleness and were responsible for attacks on native rites and religious leaders. The result was 1680 and the mass uprising of the pueblo peoples which forced the Spaniards into a 13-year exile. The reconquest by Diego de Vargas in 1693 was far from moderate and he, too, failed to observe many of the laws, especially those concerning land right. But after his two administrations, a real modus vivendi between Spaniard and Pueblo Indian developed and by and large, most laws were enforced when the pueblos took their cases against Spaniards directly to the authorities. Occupation and conquest are never without pain, whatever the outcome. Credit for finally evolving coexistence as a way of life in spite of all vicissitudes throughout the Colonial period belongs of course to both groups, Hispanic and Pueblo Indian.

# NOTES

1. George P. Hammond and Agapito Rey, *Don Juan de Onate, Colonizer of New Mexico, 1595-1628* (Albuquerque, 1953), I, p. 322. The name of "San Juan de los Caballeros" is given by Villagra writing some twelve years after the fact, but it does not appear in the contemporary documents. See: Gilberto Espinosa nd F.W. Hodge, trans. and eds., *History of New Mexico by Gaspar Perez de Villagra* (Los Angeles; 1933), p. 147.

2. Hammond and Rey, *Don Juan de Onate*, I, p. 323.

3. *Ibid.*, pp. 17 and 609, fn. Although the editors make this statement in the introduction to their monumental work, no reference to a move is found in the documents which they include.

4. *Ibid.*, II, pp. 608-609.

5. *Ibid.*, II, pp. 644, 652.

6. *Ibid.*, I, pp. 5-16; 42-336.

7. Myra Ellen Jenkins, "Spanish Land Grants in the Tewa Area," *New Mexico Historical Review*, vol. 47 (1972), p. 113.

8. Leslie Byrd Simpson, *The Encomienda in New Spain* (Berkeley, 1950), p. 129.

9. *Ibid.*, p. 145; C.H. Haring, *The Spanish Empire in America* (New York, 1947), pp. 55-60; Lewis Hanke, *The Spanish Struggle for Justice in the Conquest of America* (Philadelphia, 1949), pp. 48-67.

10. Haring, *Spanish Empire*, pp. 64-68; Charles Gibson, *Spain in America* (New York, 1966), pp. 143-147.

11. *Recopilacion de leyes de los reynos de las Indias.* (Madrid, 1681), Book IV, title 12, law 5.

12. *Recop.*, Book IV, title 12, law 14 and title 12, law 9.

13. *Recop.*, Book IV, title 12, law 18.

14. Gibson, *Spain in America*, pp. 197-198; Henry W. Kelly, "Franciscan Missions of New Mexico, 1740-1760," NMHR, vol. 15 (1940), pp. 349-350.

15. "Ordenanzas de Su Magestad Hechas para laos Descubrimiento, Conquistas y Pacificaciones, Julio de 1573," *Coleccion de Documentos Ineditos Relativos al descubrimiento, Conquista Y Organizacion de Las Antiguas Posessiones Espanoles de America y Oceania Sacados de los Archivos del Reino . . .* (Madrid, 1871), vol. 16, pp. 142-187.

16. Hammond and Rey, *Don Juan de Onate*, I, p. 65.

17. *Ibid.*, pp. 342-347.

18. David H. Snow, "A Note on Encomienda Economics in Seventeenth Century New Mexico," in Marta Weigle, ed., *Hispanic Arts and Ethnohistory in the Southwest* (Santa Fe, 1983), p. 349.

19. Charles Wilson Hackett, ed., *Historical Documents Relating to New Mexico, Nueva Vizcaya, and Approaches Thereto, to 1773, Collected by Adolph F. Bandelier and Fanny Bandelier* (Washington, D.C.), vol. 3, p. 120.

20. Ordenanzas, 1573, p. 182.

21. Myra Ellen Jenkins, "Spanish Colonial Administration and the Pueblo of Ysleta del Sur," report introduced as evidence for plaintiff in Ysleta del Sur vs. the United States, United States Indian Claims Commission, Washington, D.C., 1970, pp. 24-25.

22. Hammond and Rey, *Don Juan de Onate*, I, pp. 428-430. The full account is found on pp. 428-429; Villagra gave a vividly detailed but somewhat exaggerated account. See: Espinosa, *Villagra's Historia*, pp. 196-267.

23. Hammond and Rey, *Don Juan de Onate*, II, pp. 649, 1127-1128.

24. *Ibid.*, I, 447-449.

25. *Ibid.*, II, pp. 649, 1129.

26. *Ibid.*, II, pp. 650-651.

27. *Ibid.*, II, pp. 1109-1115.

# THE NEW PUEBLO ECONOMY
## *Richard I. Ford*

Don Juan Onate and his convoy of adventurous soldiers and servants lived in a world of patron-client social relations, material wealth, iron tools, food markets, domesticated animals, Aristotelian logic, divine right and blessing. The Tewa whose land they chose to colonize could not have been more different. They were subsistence farmers and foragers, hunters not herders, admirers of sacred wisdom not social dominance, employers of stone tools and animism. In the Pueblos, Onate's prelate discovered "here corn is God,"[1] worship brought rain and toil produced this grain. While seeking silver and Christian souls, these Spanish colonists were reluctant farmers more accustomed to food plundered from others.[2] Despite the contrast in their world views, Onate and his followers brought new seeds for life, new varieties of maize, wheat, and vegetables and the tools for environmental destruction, iron axes and livestock — and the Pueblo people accepted them. The ecology of the upper Rio Grande valley would be changed forever.

Human adaptation to any environment involves a complex array of decisions based upon culturally defined perceptions. Each culture "sees" the world through a different pair of cultural glasses. This relativistic view of ecological transaction is even more apparent when one culture is an immigrant into the land of another. Adaptation, then, is a dynamic adjustment by a culture to biological populations, plant and animal; to the natural environment and most importantly to other cultures. Some ecological situations are controlled by the vicissitudes of climate. Humans, particularly foragers, must adjust to unexpected weather with seasonal movements or the use of storage facilities. Agriculturalists, on the other hand, are not immune from climatic change, but they can often regulate their ecosystem by raising crops in favorable locations, by encouraging field plants, and even by altering nature with water control, or irrigation, and terracing. Nevertheless, two human cultures may not prosper equally in the same land because their cultural adjustments to the world are so different. The Spanish immigrants' and Tewa residents' contrasting ecological relationships are illustrative of different economic success and survival.

Onate and a select group of soldiers preceded the main column of colonists, carritas, and livestock to the Tewa villages at the

73

confluence of the Rio Grande and Chama on July 11, 1598.[3] Even before the others arrived and took residence on August 18, the soldiers a week earlier constructed a large irrigation canal with the assistance of some 1500 Indians.[4] An acequia was imperative if there would be wheat to replenish their depleted stores the next year. Although the degree of aboriginal irrigation is not mentioned, the Spanish certainly commented on the rainfall agriculture practiced regularly by the Tewa and took advantage of their cultural precept to store several years of corn in anticipation of drought or crop loss.[5] The Spanish also brought seed for kitchen gardens and orchards, both unkown to the Tewa. Moreover, before departing Mexico Onate passed his final inspection with herd animals: sheep, goats, cattle, ox, and horses. The number that survived consumption en route is not documented but it appears significant. These animals also had to eat and the grassy hillsides were adequate for breeding stock. The inventory also reveals iron axes for cutting fuel and constructing buildings,[6] the first being a small church completed in September. The Spanish, in other words, introduced the plants, animals, and tools that could quickly alter the landscape.

In contrast, the resident Tewa subsisted on maize supplemented with squash, beans, and gathered plant products. Their meat came from communal hunts for rabbits and hares, and from deer and other game. Firewood was already deadwood rather than cut trees and construction timbers were readily reused from older structures. This was an ecosystem which could rapidly recover when fields were abandoned or when the human population founded a new village elsewhere.

No matter what the subsistence base may be, a local area is rarely immune from unpredicted environmental challenges. In the state political system the Spanish imposed in Mexico, they could overcome subsistence problems by purchasing food in periodic markets which attracted vendors from a wide region. They also taxed farmers in produce throughout the hegemony and could provision from these stores those elites with special need. Of course, this was at the Indian peasant's expense. Lacking markets or a regional government the individual Pueblo in New Mexico solved its occasional food problems by ceremonial redistribution within the village and by trading with other Pueblos and, as the Spanish recorded, with nomads on the Plains from whom they obtained bison robes and dried meat in exchange for corn and cotton fabrics. With the arrival of the Spanish the absence of markets meant the securing of foodstuff from the Pueblos with whom they

74

had contact and even to the detriment of the Indians' well-being as disgruntled colonists reported at the Valverde inquest of 1601.[7] For instance, one witness swore:

> ". . . *every year armed soldiers and even the governor go in person from house to house to collect a blanket from each house or each Indian. Those who do not have one give a buckskin. The Indians, because of their poverty, part with these things with much feeling. Furthermore, every time the Spaniards need maize, they go after it and get it without payment or giving anything in trade.*"[8]

Our concern is with the adaptions the Tewa populations had to make to the presence of the Spanish in New Mexico. In order to determine these we must examine historically and ecologically the new plants introduced by the Spanish and the methods they used to raise them. The role of herd animals will be considered separately. Before reaching a conclusion we must review the documentary record, the archaeological evidence, and ethnography of the Tewa. Only then can we appreciate the ecological implications of a changing ecosystem and the new economic adjustments made by the Tewa.

## Documentary Evidence

Onate wished to depart for New Mexico shortly after receiving his contract in September, 1595. Political intrigue and bureaucratic inertia delayed his expedition and resulted in two major inspections for compliance with his contract. The inventory of most items (though not all) was recorded and these listings become our first detailed summary of the new plants and animals the Spanish would introduce to the Pueblo lands. Previously, Gaspar Castano de Sosa had brought corn and wheat from Mexico for his followers, but between September and December, 1590, most of the seed was consumed as hunger stalked the expedition.[9] What happened to the last *fanegas* of wheat saved for planting is unknown but they apparently were not sown in New Mexico.

The inventory by Don Lope de Ulloa y Lemos in Santa Barbara, Chihuahua, in 1596 and 1597 is most informative. Onate had procured 312 *fanegas* of corn, some 12 *fanegas* of beans, and 500 *fanegas* of wheat seed. Most of these were probably consumed during the subsequent delay of the expedition's departure. But the medicine box recorded at this time survived for the trip northward and it contained beans, barley, and lentils, most likely in flour form, for plasters. Its medicinal herbs were camomile, dill, rue, *estafiate* (an *Artemisia*), and marshmallow (probably *Malva* sp.).[10]

A second inventory by Juan de Frias Salazar beginning in 1597 revealed wheat, corn flour, iron hoes, and significantly numerous axes "for chopping firewood."[11] The domesticated animals which would provide food en route and breeding stock in New Mexico included 846 goats, 198 oxen, 2517 sheep, 383 rams, 96 colts, 101 mares, and 41 mules and jackasses. Sixteen potential colonists brought additional animals.

After the colony was established Onate sought new recruits and replenishment of supplies. The Gordejuela Inspection of 1600 is very instructive for a variety of foods and their potential as new plants to be grown in New Mexico. The luxury items suggest that orchards, if planted by the original colonists, were not yet producing as quince and peach preserves, raisins, almonds, olives and walnuts were shipped. Also sent were the herbs and spices anise, rosemary, lavender, wild marjoram, and coriander. Some of these may have been added to the gardens at least some of the Spanish established.[13]

In the first decade of the fledgling colony investigations of dissension and exploitation of the Indians produced scores of documents describing the conditions of the colonists and their agrarian activities in particular. In his undocumented *History of New Mexico*, Villagra proclaimed the Spanish gave the Pueblos lettuce, cabbage, peas, chickpeas, cumin-seed, carrots, turnips, garlic, onions, artichokes, radishes, and cucumbers.[14] By reading this list we learn that the officially inspected inventories did not include food items not originally contracted by Onate. Apparently, garden vegetables were ignored. The land was acknowledged by all as fertile and productive. Onate and his loyal followers praised the gardens full of Castilian vegetables and fruits, the success of the 3000 cattle and sheep grazing in New Mexico, and the spring wheat harvest.[15] They experienced an annual increase in wheat starting with a paltry seven *fanegas* planted in 1599, the next year 50 *fanegas* yielded almost 1000 *fanegas,* and an estimated 1500 *fanegas* in 1601. A letter sent from San Gabriel before 1601 and cited by Torquemado summarized the irrigation farming situation.

*Irrigation water [from the chama] was used for fields of wheat and barley and maize . . . and all other things that were planted in gardens because in that land are . . . cabbages, onions, lettuces, radishes, and other small garden stuff . . . many good melons and watermelons [sandias] . . . wheat, maize, and Mexican chile all do well.*[17]

There was another side to Onate's venture as revealed

by the testimony of those who fled this alleged tyrant. But even their complaints are instructive about farming methods in San Gabriel. Even if the gardens did not meet their expectations, they served another purpose. "The people leave their houses to sleep in their small vegetable gardens (in summer) in order to escape the unbearable plague of bedbugs."[18] Other complaints included difficulties raising the crops. "The mice eat the chile and peppers so fast that if the latter are not harvested in time the mice do not leave anything; they do not eat cheese."[19] Life must have, indeed, been trying for these soldiers of fortune.

The list of plants provided in Onate's inventories and by the colonists' testimonies was augmented by only a few additions when Benavides wrote his general description of New Mexico 35 years later. They were lentils, broad beans, lima beans, and vetches. More significant was his specific mention of plums, apricots, and peaches. These are tree crops that could be grown in orchards or as fence row fruit supplements. He also observed that "so fertile is the land that it has been seen to harvest a hundred and twenty, and a hundred and thirty, fanegas to [each] fanega sown of wheat,"[20] figures even Onate's hyperbole could not approach.

These historical documents, however, do not resolve one of the perennial problems in southwestern ethnobotany: when were melons (watermelon and cantaloupe) first introduced? Castano's journal never mentions melons but Onate and his literate followers observed them in use when they reconnoitered the Indian villages along the Rio Grande corridor and westward. All four witnesses at the valverde inquest mention melons and watermelons in a matter of fact manner. Speaking of San Gabriel one stated

*The people devote themselves to agriculture, growing maize, beans, calabashes, fine melons, and watermelons.*[21]

Another testified

*These people are farmers. They grow maize, cotton, beans, calabashes, melons, and watermelons.*[22]

Still another repeated most items on this list: "They plant maize, beans, cotton, calabashes, melons, and other things."[23] The last swore that they raise ". . . maize, calabashes, melons, watermelons, and other fruits that he saw . . ."[24] Finally, earlier in March, 1599, Onate, while extolling the general virtues of New Mexico noted both plants.

*There are fine grape vines, rivers, and woods, with many oak and some cork trees; there are also fruits, melons, grapes, watermelons, Castilian plums, capulins, pinon, acorns, native nuts, corolejo, which is a delicate fruit, and other wild plants.* [25]

It appears that watermelons and a cantaloupe-type melon were introduced to some Pueblos in the seven years before Onate established his colony.

Admittedly, the observers could have mistaken the green striped cushaw squash (*Cucurbita mixta*) or bottle gourd for watermelons and melons, respectively, but I doubt it. In the absence of distribution of seed by Coronado's expedition or subsequent *entradas,* a more likely explanation is that the seeds were dispersed from Mexican Indians living on the Conchas River who Espejo observed to possess them by 1582. [26] Considering the trade networks throughout the Southwest and the lack of abundant sweet fruits in any Pueblo economy, melons could have been spread rather quickly. Since they would have followed traditional routes of transmission, this explanation would also account for most Pueblo cultures maintaining that watermelon was pre-Hispanic in their cultures because until the establishment of Onate's colony no European plants had been introduced by non-Indians into the Southwest.

The documents are ambiguous about the degree and rate of acceptance of European crops by the Pueblos. Onate informed his relatives in 1601:

*Our wheat has been sown and harvested it does extremely well in that land. The Indians devote themselves willingly to its cultivation.* [27]

But he was referring not to the wheat planted for Indians but for the Spanish under the encomienda system of production permitted by the Council of the Indies and taken full advantage of by Onate. The only hint given in the early documents to Pueblo people sowing wheat is a comment by the Onate loyal colonist, Captain Alonso Gomez Montesinos, who ". . . estimated the amount of grain that would be harvested (in 1601) at fifteen hundred fanegas of wheat, which, with a little more from the natives . . ." [28] Likewise, the Onate documents do not mention the Pueblos raising gardens with European vegetables. However, Villagra does suggest the early adoption of gardens by the Pueblos.

In summary the historical documents do list a substantial variety of introduced plants of both Mexican and European origin. They also reveal the introduction of kitchen gardens as a new method to raise vegetables. They state that the Pueblos used both dry farming and irrigation with irrigation water essential for a successful wheat crop. By the time of Benevides' observations, at least, orchard trees of plum, peaches, and apricots were yielding fruit. The documents also emphasize the rapid growth of sheep and cattle herds to over 3000 animals in the vicity of San Gabriel and San Juan. Overall numerous forces for ecological change and adaptive contrast confronted these Pueblos with the initial colonization of their land.

## Archaeological Evidence

Data recovered from archaeological sites can complement the historical record. They can show the distribution of new crops from Pueblos which the documents may not mention and archeobotanical evidence can resolve ambiguities with reference to specific plant identifications. Several Spanish-introduced plants will be examined to assess their particular distribution and to determine which of these plants the Pueblos actually grew for their consumption.

In archaeology the techniques used to excavate a site will determine the amount and variety of the plant remains recovered. Regrettably, neither screens nor flotation (water separation) methods were used to recover animal bones or charred plant parts when Yunque was dug in the early 1960s. In fact, prior to 1970 few historic contact sites had been excavated with equipment appropriate for retrieval of plant and animal evidence. Some remains had been found by hand in the fill, and although these are meager and bias samples, they are helpful and compare favorably with the documents. More recently, excellent methods were used by archaeologists at the Palace of the Governors in Santa Fe and at Walpi.

Prehistoric plant remains reveal the Pueblo IV Rio Grande inhabitants grew a short cob 10-12 row corn, common beans (*Phaseolus vulgaris*), bottle gourds (*Laginaria siceraria*), two species of squashes (*Cucurbita pepo* and *C. mixta*), and cotton (*Gossypium hirstutum* var. *punctatum*). They gathered pinon nuts, prickly pear cactus, yucca fruits, juniper berries, pigweed (*Amaranthus* sp.) goosefoot (*Chenopodium* sp.) seeds, and purslane (*Portulaca retusa*).

Archaeobotanical evidence does not resolve the watermelon and muskmelon/cantaloupe dating problem other than to show the widespread distribution of these sweet fruits before the Pueblo Rebellion. Watermelon seeds from historic turkey pens at Abo Mission suggest the cultivation of two horticultural varieties. Muskmelon/cantaloupe were found in the same context.[29] Further west, watermelon seeds were recognized in two historic contexts at Hawikuh.[30] Adobe bricks formed for building the Franciscan mission at Awatovi upon being wet yielded numerous watermelon and cantaloupe seeds.[31]

Another poorly dated fruit of general distribution is the peach (*Prunus persica*). Peach pits were common in the historic levels at Awatovi and again at Abo.[32] They were present in the 17th century at Puaray,[33] Paa-ko,[34] and Picuris.[35] Two additional sites, Pecos[36] and Jemez Cave,[37] produced peach pits but perhaps from later chronological contexts.

Abo and Awatovi provided remains of several other European domesticates. Wheat and apricot pits were found in the adobe bricks from the Franciscan mission.[38] Wine grape pips (*Vitis vinfera*), European plum pits (*Prunus domesticus*), coriander seeds (*Coriandrum sativum*), and chile pepper parts (*Capsicum annum*) all came from Abo.[39] The coriander and chile are the earliest authenticated evidence for these important garden crops in the Pueblo area.

Recently the interior of the Palace of the Governors was renovated. Before the installation of new floors and walls, the sub-surface deposits were excavated. A number of large pits were opened and they yielded an exceptional array of European plant remains. These included plum, peach, apricot, cherry, watermelon, cultivated grape, wheat, and perhaps barley (*Hordeum vulgare*). Two noteworthy tree products were hazelnut (*Corvlus* sp.) and English walnut (*Juglans regia*). Neither tree is known to have been grown by the early Spanish in New Mexico and they may have been brought as luxury items from Mexico where they were grown or they may have been gathered more recently by rodents living under the old floors. In either case Seifert interprets these pits as probably fill dumped by Spanish occupants after they reoccupied the Palace following the Pueblo Rebellion. Indians may not have grown or consumed them although the remains are extremely important for the crop history of New Mexico.[40]

The actual use of these European introduced plants by Pueblo Indians is a problem. Even if the areas of the site which yielded the plants were occupied by Indians, their immediate proximity to Spanish domiciles does not mean the Indians raised them for personal consumption.

The actual eating and probably production of these new crops was only recently resolved by the excavation of Walpi Pueblo at Hopi. For the first time European domesticated plants were recovered outside a Spanish mission-associated site and away from a Spanish presence in the regions. Here the Post-Rebellion, Payupki period, dating from A.D. 1690 to A.D. 1800, component has associated with it most of the plants found elsewhere, only this time from a single site: watermelon, cantaloupe, peach, apricot, plum, cherry, and chile. A new addition to the overall list of garden plants is the onion (*Allium cepa*).[41]

Beyond the European cultigens, the Spanish also introduced a number of plants domesticated elsewhere in the Americans. Chile peppers from Mexico were first brought to the American Southwest by the Spanish. They also transported new varieties of corn such as the large cob, Cristalina de Chihuahua corn and the high-rowed Mexican dent from highland Mexico. At one time it was felt these were prehistoric cultivars of the Pueblos but work at Picuris clarified the correct chronolgy to a 17th century introduction.[42] They also brought Hubbard squash (*Cucurbita maxima*) from South America as revealed by seeds from Picuris and undoubtedly elsewhere during the same century.[43]

Equally significant is the New World, non-food plant, *Nicotiana rustica* or tobacco, also called *punche* by the Spanish. One documentary reference to the early used tobacco by the Spanish does not specify the species although it suggests one available in quantity and familiar to the settlers. *N. rustica* was the most frequently smoked tobacco in Mexico at the time of contact. It was most likely introduced to New Mexico. Zarate Salmeron's passing remark is most significant concerning the tobacco problem.

> The Spaniards who are there (New Mexico) laugh at all this (i.e., accusations of laziness); as long as they have a good supply of tobacco to smoke, they are very contented, and they do not want any more riches, for it seems as if they had made a vow of poverty.[44]

Archaeological evidence indicates that *N. rustica* was introduced to New Mexico before 1680 because its large leaves and seed capsules were found in a historic Tewa red bowl from the Pueblo Rebellion reoccuaption of the Bandelier cliff dwellings.[45] The indigenous, white flowered tobacco, *N. attenuata*, is still collected wild and used by the Pueblos; *punche*, the yellow-flowered N. rustica, used to be grown on the edge of fields or in Pueblo gardens.

Some questons remain about the introduction of two other plants to the Pueblos. Sweet corn was not grown prehistorically in the upper Rio Grande Valley but was also grown in the Mexican highlands of Chihuahua and was brought at sometime to New Mexico. Since the documents rarely provide varietal names in Spanish (a *maiz duce* is not recorded) and since archaeological evidence is lacking, we know little about when it was introduced.

Domesticated amaranth is likewise an unresolved problem. Its scientific name is *Amaranthus hypochondriacus* and it provides edible leaves and abundant seeds for porridge. It is known prehistorically from Tonto in southern Arizona and has recently been reported in prehistoric contexts from Pot Creek north of Picuris. Yet it was not grown or reported specifically when the Spanish arrived in San Juan or Picuris and there is no ethnographic evidence for it until this century when it was grown as an ornamental. Throughout the historical period non-domesticated amaranth was cultivated and double harvested for a potherb and seed. The available amaranth seeds from ar-cheological sites are burned and prohibit a species designation.

Although the documentary and archaeobotanical records are incomplete, they do provide complementary testimony to the great number of plants brought by the Spanish beginning with Onate. While most green leafy vegetables and three European beans have not been found by archaeologists, the other plants mentioned in historical sources have been and from a broad area. The evidence from archaeological sites has also resolved the species identification of several Spanish derived plants. The Walpi excavations suggest that European plants and the garden technology were accepted by the Pueblos certainly within a century after contact.

## Ethnographic Evidence

The processes for integrating Spanish-introduced crops into the traditional Tewa economy remain unexplored. A brief analysis of Tewa linguistic terms, cuisine preferences, and ritual are instructive, however.

Wheat has been accorded special status when compared to the other plants. Wheat bread baked in beehive outdoor ovens accompanies all religious festivities; wheat seed blessed by the Summer Cacique is included in the ceremonial shinny ball played prior to planting to assure a bountiful harvest throughout the farm land. The Tewa term for wheat, *tata*, is not a borrowing of the Spanish, *trigo*, and suggests an early acceptance and indeed dependence upon wheat. The Tewa name may be derivved from *tatan*, 'grass seed,' based upon its morphology and useful seed.

Several of the first introduced vegetables and fruits were nam-ed by analogy with known plants. Thus peas are *tutsanbe*, 'white bean fruit'; *tu* meaning bean. *Be* is a round fruit and is used for apples. But it is also a stem as in *bef'o'in*, 'hairy fruit,' the peach; *bepi'in*, 'red fruit,' the apricot, plum, or prune. The general term for onion, *si*, has been transferred to the domesticated onion. True root crops have the stem *pu* for root and adjectival describer of their color or flavor: *pupi'in* 'red root,' beet; *putsaein* 'white root,' turnip; *putse'in* 'yellow root,' obviously the carrot; and *pusaein*, 'hot root,' or a radish.

Most other fruits and vegetables are named according to a borrowed Spanish term. Chile cannot be prehispanic in origin since the Tewa call it *tsindi*, a variant of Spanish, *chile*. *Sandia* is the term for watermelon in Tewa as it is in Spanish. *Kole* (Span. *col*) for cabbage and *letsuga* (Span. *lechuga*) for lettuce. Borrowed names for fruits are also common: *uba* (Span. *uva*), grape; *seresia* (Span. *cereza*), cherry; *oliba* (Span. *oliva*), olive; *Kulantu* (Span. *Culantro*), coriander; and *pera* (Span. *pera*), pear. *Merikanuto*, 'American nut' or *Kakawate*, Span. *cacahuate*,) terms for the recently introduced peanut.[46]

In addition to their borrowed names, the introduced fruit contrast in the food classification system used by the Tewa. Indigenous fruits are generally conceived as "hot but those from outside are "cold," a potential source of illness or at least diarrhea if consumed in great quantity.

The Spanish brought corn obtained in the northern highlands of Mexico. This dramatic large cobbed corn was conspicuously more productive and was quickly bred by the Pueblos but according to Tewa color categories. Color is the major classificatory scheme of Tewa corn to satisfy both ritual prescriptions and culinary expectations. The colors — blue, yellow, red, white — never changed;indeed the traditional system guided acceptance of new corn as the size of the cob and a slight dent in many kernels reveal genetic introgression with the Mexican derived corn.

Finally, the large fruit and sweet taste of sandia are good symbols of a prosperous harvest. They are prominent in the Harvest Dance, often broken on Mother Earth. Public performances of Kossa are complete with the watermelon. Watermelons are favorite gifts for friends, a refreshing repast for dancers, and an appropriate offering to the deceased on the Day of the Dead (November 2).

Tewa ethnography confirms the historic documentary history of crop introductions and the culturally directed integration of fruits and vegetables into the food system and language and of corn genes into the ancient staple grain. The appearance of plants in rituals reinforces the history of each plant and the partitioning of indigenous from introduced food. Only watermelon, wheat, and chile have special significance. Except for its name, watermelon is treated as an aboriginal food. Wheat and chile are used in some agricultural ceremonies, but not all. The other plants are treated separately, and are given no role in traditional rites; their foreign-origin status is retained linguistically and ritually even after 380 years!

## Ecological Consequences

Onate and his followers reached San Juan in July with ample time to construct an irrigation ditch within a month. They brought spring wheat so it was not until the following year that the Spanish demonstrated a new technology that the Indians would soon adopt: plowed fields, irrigated wheat, and kitchen gardens for vegetables and herbs.

Wheat was an excellent complement to corn. Planted when the frost left the ground and harvested in July or August, wheat presented no work schedule conflict with maize. Moreover, corn was planted mostly in scattered dry-farm fields, some in arroyos away from the flood plain. Wheat was concentrated on bottomland accessible to irrigation water. Here it did not displace the corn. The vagaries of climate, even during the Little Ice Age recently discussed by Simmons,[47] might have adversely affected one crop one season but not necessarily both corn and wheat. Wheat became the high yield caloric safety value in the Pueblo economy. Its cultivation demanded only a reliable supply of irrigation water.

Kitchen gardens were a new innovation. Grown with irrigation water as a polyculture in a confined space, they added great variety to the Pueblo diet and became the dietary complement to gathered wild plants. The difference from foraging was that the yield of gardens was greater than the natural occurrence of weedy species like amaranth, goosefoot, and purslane in the fields and by concentrating them in one location, they were easier to harvest. Certainly the European vegetables amplified the Tewa economy without a major technological modification of the arable land.

Orchards were established and were yielding peach, apricot, plum, and cherries before 1630. They were probably established by Onate's colonists but the early documents are mute about them. Nevertheless, the trees could be planted off the prime arable land thus expanding the productivity of marginal land.

By the 19th century the Tewa had a settlement pattern with

scattered summer field houses located by irrigation ditches and surrounded by kitchen gardens and fruit trees. Those who stayed in the village after San Juan Day (June 24), the traditional time others moved to their field houses, planted gardens along the eastern canal and fruit trees along their field boundaries on the west side of the village. When the pattern of field house-garden-orchard evolved is unknown. The potential and indeed the economic necessity for this pattern was enabled by the Spanish introduced technology. Together they increased the productivity of the land.

Herd animals had a double-edged impact on the Tewa. On the one hand, they became a source for meat, textile material, and beasts of burden. The meat was available for ceremonial feasts or when hunting was inopportune. Although cotton was grown in the upper Rio Grande, it was marginal and not always successful. Wool was more plentiful and available for textiles, though it never assumed the ceremonial significance cotton is still accorded. Moreover, with firewood scarce in the immediate vicinity of the Pueblos, burros, mules, and horses became available to carry back loads of fuel from several miles away which had previously been cumbersome and time consuming when human backs were the means of transport.

On the other hand, stock could quickly overgraze the grass, trample young tree seedlings, and compact the land. Stock also could enter cultivated land, especially outlying fields required by the Pueblos for corn. A similar situation confronted Indian communities in the Valle del Mezquital north of Mexico City. There overgrazing within 30 years led to environmental degradation and a reduction by half of palatable grass.[48]

In New Mexico, mining and ranching became two economic enterprises for the Spanish colonists. Right from the beginning by 1601 the initial herd of breeding stock grew to 3000 sheep and cattle. Three decades later Benavides commented about the behavior of governors in New Mexico who made grants of Indian land for cattle and who established profitable ranches of their own.

*They (grantees) force the Indians, by evil treatment and by losses to their cattle, to abandon their lands and to leave their possessions to the Spaniards.*

*. . . And in order to send their (governors') cattle to New Spain to sell, they rob the land of the cattle which are so desirable for increasing its welfare and permanence . . . With their connivance others, too, send out cattle, and in particular female cattle, whereby*

*the land is impoverished.* [49]

With the expansion of the pastoral economy the potential deleterious effects of overgrazing — arroyo formation, a conversion to short grass prairies, lowered water table, and the loss of native economic plants — cannot be ignored. The grazing of sheep and cattle on both Indian land and on seemingly unoccupied "free" land would have brought rapid ecological destruction and must be given more attention.

A final agent for manifest ecological change was the metal axe. Onate's colonists each had several. The Tewa have traditionally collected dead limbs rather than live trees for firewood. The iron axe in the hands of the Spanish permitted the felling of large trees. Mature cottonwood, juniper, and pinon were all vulnerble to its bite as the new settlers collected wood for warmth and cooking. By the 19th century the land surrounding San Juan was virtually bereft of trees. Cottonwoods did not line the river bands and the farm village called New York was visible from the Pueblo of San Juan. Only a few scattered juniper trees were found anywhere on the land grant. Not on pinon was to be seen. When the reservation boundary was surveyed by the United States Government in the 1850s, most trees were gone, the land was desecrated from grazing, and erosion had advanced markedly. Axes and animals had denuded the land. [50]

## The New Pueblo Economy

One prehistoric means for coping with political disputes, lack of firewood, or unproductive fields was migration. The new economic base of the Pueblos gave the means for long term inhabitation in the face of adversity. The several fold increase in domesticated plant species was a source of a beneficial and more secure subsistence base. Wheat, kitchen vegetable gardens, and orchards were welcome additions. Draft animals permitted easier access to distant sources for wood, and riding animals opened new hunting grounds on the eastern plains. The new economy increased the yield from traditional homelands.

To abandon a village after the first few decades of contact became difficult if not impossible because of the Spanish imposed political system. But the necessity resulting from environmental calamity was mitigated by the expanded economic base. Integrated according to Tewa cultural values the new plants and animals safeguarded against ecolgical disaster. While the Spanish complained of food scarcity and the colonists were reluctant to

86

accept the native foods the Tewa ate, their Pueblo neighbors were adopting the new food, expanding their control over the productivity of their land, and building economic security.

The new Pueblo economy did not change the traditional Tewa way of life. If anything it reinforced it, gave material substantiation to it, and enabled the cultural continuity the living descendants of the first people permanently to host the Spanish enjoy today.

Cultural ecology is a complex subject. The Tewa experience at San Juan demonstrates that some cultures, as this one has, have the ability to adopt new items from donor cultures, use them to advantage, so that the culture need not change. Even as the landscape deteriorated, the new food and increased productivity of the arable land only served to reinforce the adaptive capacity of Tewa culture. The success of San Juan Pueblo is a lesson for all of us.

# NOTES

1. George P. Hammond and Agapito Rey (eds.), *Don Juan de Onate, Colonizer of New Mexico: 1595-1628* ("Coronado Cuarto Centennial Publications, 1540-1940," Vol. V, VI; Albuquerque: University of New Mexico Press, 1953), p. 692.
2. *Ibid.*
3. *Ibid.*, p. 320.
4. *Ibid.*, pp. 322-323.
5. *Ibid.*, p. 693.
6. *Ibid.*, p. 240. Although the inventory of iron implements Alonso de Sosa presented of the Salazar Inspection in Mexico was more complete than others he brought five axes, eight hoes, thirty sickles, two saws, and a variety of chisels, adzes, wedges, and hammers.
7. *Ibid.*, pp. 640-667. In July 1601 Don Francisco de Valverde investigated charges made by a colonist who deserted Onate and New Mexico.
8. *Ibid.*, p. 667.
9. Albert H. Schroeder and Dan S. Matson, *A Colony on the Move* (Santa Fe: School of American Research, 1965), pp. 60-74.
10. Hammond and Rey, *op. cit.*, p. 106. Camomile was planted in New Mexico. It has escaped from cultivation and may be found in the Jemez Mountains.
11. *Ibid.*, p. 232.
12. *Ibid.*, pp. 215, 300-301.
13. *Ibid.*, pp. 523-551. Coriander is grown in all the Pueblos and is the most widely used herb introduced by the Spanish.
14. Gaspar Perez de Villagra, *History of New Mexico*, trans. Gilberto Espinoza ("The Quivira Society," Vol. IV; Lancaster: Lancaster Press, 1933), p. 144.
15. Hammond and Rey, *op. cit.*, p. 704.
16. George P. Hammond, "Don Juan de Onate and the Founding of New Mexico," *Historical Society of New Mexico, Publications in History*, II (October, 1927), 154.
17. Juan de Torquemada, *Monarquia Indians* (3 vols.; Madrid: Nicolas Rodriguez Franco 1723), p. 678.
18. Hammond and Rey, *op. cit.*, p. 656.
19. *Ibid.*
20. Mrs. Edward E. Ayer (trans.), *The Memorial of Fray Alonso de Venavides 1630* (Albuquerque: Horn and Wallace, Publishers, 1965), p. 36.
21. Hammond and Rey, *op. cit.*, p. 626.
22. *Ibid.*, p. 634.
23. *Ibid.*, p. 645.
24. *Ibid.*, p. 660.
25. *Ibid.*, p. 484.
26. Herbert Eugene Bolton (ed.), *Spanish Explorations in the Southwest 1542-1706* (New York: Barnes & Noble, Inc., 1946), p. 170.

27. Hammond and Rey, *op. cit.*, p. 619.

28. *Ibid.*, pp. 714-715.

29. Voleny H. Jones, "Notes on Some Organic Remains from Abo Mission," *The Mission of San Gregorio de Abo* ("Monographs of the School of American Research," No. 13, Santa Fe, 1946), p. 30.

30. Watson Smith, Richard B. Woodbury, and Nathalie F. Woodbury, *The Excavation of Hawikuh by Frederick Webb Hodge: Report of the Hendricks-Hodge Expedition, 1917-1923* ("Museum of the American Indian, Heye Foundation, Contributions," Vol. 20; New York, 1966) pp. 212, 282.

31. Ross G. Montgomery, Watson Smith, and J.O. Brew, *Franciscan Awatovi: The Excavation and Conjectural Reconstruction of a 17th Century Spanish Mission Establishment at a Hopi town in Northeastern Arizona* ("Harvard University, Peabody Museum of American Archaeology and Ethnology, Papers," Vol. 36. Awatovi Expedition Reports No. 3; Cambridge, 1949) p. 88.

32. Jones, *op. cit.*, p. 49.

33. Marjorie F. Tichy, "The Archaeology of Puaray," *El Palacio*, XLVI (July, 1939), p. 161.

34. Marjorie F. Lambert, *Paa-ko, Archaeological Chronicle of an Indian Village in North-Central New Mexico* ("Monographs of the School of American Research," No. 19; Santa Fe, 1954) p. 162.

35. Hugh C. Cutler and Leonard W. Blake, *Plants from Archaeological Sites East of the Rockies* (St. Louis: Missouri Botanical Garden, 1973), p. 50.

36. Alfred V. Kidder, *The Artifacts of Pecos* ("Phillips Academy, Department of Archaeology, Southwestern Expedition, Papers," No. 6; New Haven, 1932), p. 308.

37. Hubert G. Alexander and Paul Reiter, *Report on the Excavation of Jemez Cave*, No. 4; Santa Fe, 1935), p. 64.

38. Montgomery, Watson, and Brew, *loc. cit.*

39. Jones, *op. cit.*, pp. 30-31.

40. Donna J. Seifert, *Archaeological Excavations at the Palace of the Governors, Santa Fe, New Mexico: 1974 and 1975*, Report Prepared for the History Division (Santa Fe: Museum of New Mexico, 1979), pp. 127-132.

41. E. Charles Adams, *Walpi Archaeological Project: Synthesis and Interpretation* (Flagstaff: Museum of Northern Arizona, 1982), p. 94.

42. Cutler and Blake, *loc. cit.*

43. *Ibid.*

44. Zarate Salmeron, *Relaciones*, trans. Alicia Ronstadt Milich (Albuquerque: Horn & Wallace Publishers, 1966), p. 56.

45. Specimen identified by Volney H. Jones and Richard I. Ford, 1965.

46. Wilfred William Robbins, John Peabody Harrington, and Barbara Freier-Marreco, *Ethnobotany of the Tewa Indians* ("Smithsonian Institution, Bureau of American Ethnology, Bulletin," 55; Washington, 1916), pp. 107-117.

47. Marc Simmons, "New Mexico's Colonial Agriculture," *El Palacio*, 89 (Spring 1983), p. 6.

48. Elinor Gordon Ker Melville, "The Pastoral Economy and Environmental Degradation in Highland Central Mexico, 1530-1600" (unpublished Ph.D. dissertation, Dept. of Anthropology, University of Michigan, 1983), pp. 166-210.
49. Frederick Webb Hodge, George P. Hammond, and Agapito Rey, *Fray Alonso de Benavides' Revised Memorial of 1634* ("Coronado Cuarto Centennial Publications, 1540-1940," Vd. IV: Albuquerque: University of New Mexico Press, 1945), p. 172.
50. Pueblo de San Juan, Bureau of Land Management, Public Room, Santa Fe, New Mexico. Original land survey notes.

# BIBLIOGRAPHY

Adams, E. Charles. *Walpi Archaeological Project: Synthesis and Interpretation.* Flagstaff: Museum of Northern Arizona, 1982.

Alexander, Hubert G., and Reiter, Paul. *Report on the Excavation of Jemez Cave, New Mexico.* ("Monographs of the School of the American Research," No. 4) Santa Fe, 1935.

Ayer, Mrs. Edward E. (Trans.). *The Memorial of Fray Alonso de Benavides 1630.* Albuquerque: Horn and Wallace, Publishers, 1965.

Bolton, Herbert Eugene (ed.) *Spanish Exploration in the Southwest: 1542-1706.* New York: Barnes & Noble, 1946.

Cutler, Hugh C. and Blake, Leonard W. *Plants from Archaeological Sites East of the Rockies.* St. Louis: Missouri Botanical Garden, 1973.

Hammond, George P. "Don Juan de Onate and the Founding of New Mexico," *Historical Society of New Mexico, Publications in History,* II (October, 1927), 1-228.

Hammond, George P. and Rey, Agapito (eds.) *Don Juan de Onate, Colonizer of New Mexico: 1595-1628.* ("Coronado Cuarto Centennial Publications, 1540-1940," Vol. V, VI.) Albuquerque: University of New Mexico Press, 1953.

Hodge, Frederic Webb, Hammond, George P., and Rey, Agapito. *Fray Alonso de Benavides' Revised Memorial of 1634.* ("Coronado Cuarto Centennial Publications, 1540-1940." Vol. IV.) Albuquerque: University of New Mexico Press, 1945.

Jones, Volney H. "Notes on Some Organic Remains from Abo Mission," in *The Mission of San Gregorio de Abo* ("Monographs of the School of American Research," No. 13 [Santa Fe, 1946]), 29-32.

Kidder, Alfred V. *The Artifacts of Pecos.* ("Phillips Academy, Department of Archaeology, Southwestern Expedition, Papers," No. 6.) New Haven: Yale University Press, 1932.

Lambert, Marjorie F. *Paa-ko, Archaeological Chronicle of an Indian Village in North-Central New Mexico.* ("Monographs of the School of American Research," No. 19. Santa Fe, 1954.

Melville, Elinor Gordon Ker. "The Pastoral Economy and Environmental Degradation in Highland Central Mexico, 1530-1600." Unpublished Ph.D. dissertation, University of Michigan, 1983. pp. 323.

Montgomery, Ross G., Smith, Watson, and Brew, J.O. *Franciscan Awatovi: The Excavation and Conjectural Reconstruction of a 17th century Spanish Mission Establishment at a Hopi Town in Northeastern Arizona.* ("Harvard University, Peabody Museum of American Archaeology and Ethnology, Papers," Vol. XXXVI, Awatovi Expedition Reports, No. 3) Cambridge, 1949.

Robbins, Wilfred William, Harrington, John Peabody, and Freire-Marreco, Barbara. *Ethnobotany of the Tewa Indians* ("Smithsonian Institution, Bureau of American Ethnology," Bulletin 55.) Washington, D.C.: Government Printing Office, 1916.

Schroeder, Albert H. and Watson, Dan S. *A Colony on the Move.* Santa Fe: School of American Research, 1965.

Seifert, Donna J. "Archaeological Excavations at the Palace of the Governors, Santa Fe, New Mexico: 1974 and 1975." Report prepared for the History Division, Museum of New Mexico, Santa Fe, 1979. pp. 253.

Simmons, Marc. "New Mexico's Colonial Agriculture," *El Palacio*, 89, No. 1 (Spring 1983), 3-10.

Smith, Watson, Woodbury, Richard B., and Woodbury, Nathalie F.S. *The Excavation of Hawikuh by Frederick Webb Hodge: Report of the Hendricks-Hodge Expedition, 1917-1923.* (Museum of the American Indian, Heye Foundation, Contributions," Vol. 20.) New York, 1966.

Tichy, Marjorie Ferguson. "The Archaeology of Pauray," *El Palacio*, XLVI, No. 7 (July, 1939), 145-163.

Torquemada, Juan de. *Monarquia Indiana.* 3 vols. Madrid: Nicolas Rodriguez Franco, 1723.

Villagra, Gaspar Perez de. *History of New Mexico.* Translated by Gilberto Espinosa. ("The Quivira Society," Vol. IV.) Lancaster: Lancaster Press, 1933.

Zarate Salmeron. *Relaciones.* Translated by Alicia Ronstadt Milich. Albuquerque: Horn & Wallace Publishers, 1966.

# EL TURCO, A Story
*Jim Sagel*

Soy el Turco. The "Turk" they call me, even though I've got no more Ottoman blood in my veins than your grandmother's chihuahua. But those Spaniards — heads all mushed up with Moorish devils as they were — well, soon as they got a load of my swarthy good looks, they labelled me the "Turk" and the nickname just stuck. But, then, I've never been to India either and you all call me "Indian," so what's the difference?

Esclavo me llaman tambien — they call me "slave." But he who claims to own me is a greater slave than I. Didn't they chain up my so-called "master," old Pecos Bigotes, when he dared to disagree with my tall tales? And, speaking of bigotes, who could imagine a more servile subject than the mighty bigoton himself, Francisco Vasquez de Coronado, slave to my silvery tongue and the shimmering illusion of my gold-leafed words?

Si, soy el embustero, one of history's great liars, but don't sit there so smugly — I can still trick you too. So, tell me, what do you want to hear? That's my skill, you see: I paint poems out of your dreams. I embellish the greedy underbelly of your fantasies, and the more fantastic my story, the easier it is to beguile you. You want to hear about that winning lottery ticket waiting for you at the 7 to 11 Speedway across from Colonel Sander's Kentucky Fried Chicken in Pueblo, Colorado, which has the exact numbers of the birthdate, weight and championship record of the "Manassa Mauler," Jack Dempsey? Or would you rather hear about the killing you could make in the stock market if you'd only take an early retirement from your job and cash in your insurance policies in order to get in on the ground floor of a new artificial spleen company with home offices in the outskirts of Hoboken?

No se rien. Well, go ahead and laugh if you want, but I know my material works. After all, I've got more than four centuries of experience under my belt and I know these are no fireside yarns. Feet follow my fictions — when I engage you in flights of fantasy, I'm talking airline reservations on a 747 bound for Madagascar. I mean, just consider that classic scam I ran on Corondao back in 1541. Poor pendejo was shivering that winter in the pueblito of Alcanfor, suffering from the symptoms of Cibola withdrawal syndrome — I'll tell you, he was ripe for a little gold goading. So I invented Quivira, took it straight from his romantic medieval mindset, and we may have been leagues off-Broadway, but, boy, did it play! Forget the Halls of Montezuma, I told Coronado. To the east lay an even golder kingdom, yes, the land of Quivira where there was so much gold his troops would have to rent U-hauls to cart it all away. Oh yes, Quivira, where golden bells tinkled from the boughs of stately trees at the banks of a river six miles wide where royalty serenely floated in canoes with golden prows and sipped sweet wine from silver goblets. Not bad for an amateur, no? — particularly when you consider we're talking about Kansas here. I mean, how creative can you get about Kansas? Actually, I may have waxed a little too creatively because, come spring, I was out there myself, leading Coronado and the boys dow the trail to Quivira, which called for some pretty fancy improvisation and endless variations on the old "just over the next rise" theme. The history books, of course, will tell you they executed me out there on the "lone prairee," but don't you believe it for a minute. They couldn't kill me, not as long as there was a steady supply of new fools eager to tilt at gilted windmills.

Fifty years later I was at it again, resurrecting tales of golden wonder and sending Captain Francisco Leyva de Bonilla thundering off into the sunrise. That time, I'll admit, I did accept a little kickback from the residents of San Ildefonso who had gotten sick and tired of maintaining the Spaniard on their welfare rolls. Leyva, of course, never came back, but that's not my problem — I just weave the stories and wave goodbye. I even said adios to your famous colonizer Juan de Onate when I seduced him out of his happy new home at San Gabriel and right back down that same trail through the buffalo chips and the greasy grass. By then they were calling me Jusepe or Joseph or just plain Joe, but it was really me, el Turco.

Todavia sigo mintiendo — there's more locos than ever these days who want to belive their fantasies are true because they are too blind to see how fantastic the truth really is. Do you follow me? Better not, or I'll lure you away from the river valley too. I'll snatch you from the snowy arms of the mountains and everything that's important to you and set you trudging through the empty grasslands of your heart where the horizon is endless and the future is flat and there are no directions back home. For I am the cave without a mouth, the splash of sunlight blazing adobe walls into golden fortresses. I am the rain refusing to rain. I crash anthropologists' cocktail parties and plant corn by night in the lawns of chiropracters. I play recordings of La Llorona in the bosque where the Rio Chama flows into the Rio Grande. I pretend to be

93

alive at history conferences. I built Georgia O'Keeffe's wall and I was responsible for Article VII of the Treaty of Guadalupe Hidalgo, for all that was worth. I only wish I would have never made up that insane story I told to Robert Oppenheimer because I'll be damned if that one didn't turn out to be true! I'm still busy today, convincing the heirs of Onate and Pope to become astronauts and professional basketball players, and I'm packing them into the Coronado Mall with visions of bigger and better Quiviras dancing in their heads.

¿Que dicen? — that I have the scruples of a cow stomach? Well, perhaps you haven't heard the old dicho: El que le roba a un ladron tiene cien anos de perdon — He who steals from the thief is pardoned for a hundred years. My tales lead no man where he has not already decided to go. I stay here, at the banks of my beloved rio, in the embrace of my timeless pueblo, spinning stories that simply drive the driven on by. Only problem is lately I've been stumped with all these condominium developers who scoff at my easterly stories and sniff that they've already subdivided Quivira Estates. If anyone can come up with a story idea brazen enough to mesmerize this new breed of colonizers, I'd sure appreciate hearing it. I'll be easy to spot: I'm the one who resembles a coyote in a three-piece suit. I'll be hanging around back by the door so I can be the first one out in case of a holocaust.

Mientras tanto, I'll keep searching for my favorite listeners, those who turn a deaf ear to each other. Give me those hard and intolerant men of lofty righteousness, those who pray by rote and never question the king, the men who really want to get ahead in life. As long as I have breath and wits, I'll keep making up my outrageous stories to urge them farther on, far away from my peaceful home by the river.

# WHAT BLOODS
## *Jim Sagel*

What bloods began to intermingle
    as the new century dawned

Oceany blood fluid and tidal
                    blood
that always flows to a farther shore

Earthy blood whole and primal
                    blood
that feed roots evolving into light

Holy blood raining from the mountains
                    of Christ

Sacred blood cresting in the womb
                  of the kiva

Blood of the uplifted sword
    regal and unyielding
Blood of the ripening corn
    clothed in raw silk

Blood of rust and the virgin flow
Blood of two hemispheres rushing head on

Blood of the conquerors
                and blood of those never
conquered

Alpha Anasazi Omega
            These bloods are one

**HERMAN AGOYO** – Tribal Administrator of San Juan Pueblo. He was formerly (1970-1979) the Executive Director of the Eight Northern Indian Pueblos Council. In 1980 he was Director of the Pueblo Revolt Tricentennial Celebration Project.

**LYNNWOOD BROWN** – Tribal Planner and Co-Director of the San Gabriel History Project.

**FLORENCE HAWLEY ELLIS** – Archaeologist who began work in the Southwest in 1927. She is known for her work in archaeological site dating based on tree-ring analysis and pottery classification. She has published over two hundred articles in scholarly and popular journals. Now retired from the University of New Mexico Anthropology Department, Dr. Ellis has continued her study of sites in the Gallina area. A museum at Ghost Ranch in Abiquiu, New Mexico has been named in her honor.

**RICHARD I. FORD** – Ethnobotanist who has done extensive research on the ethnobotany and human ecology of the Pueblos. Author of three books and numerous articles, Dr. Ford is on the faculty of the University of Michigan at Ann Arbor.

**MYRA ELLEN JENKINS** – Historian who has acted as an expert witness in Indian land claims cases and prepared land histories. She has served as a visiting professor at the University of New Mexico and the College of Santa Fe. From 1960-1980 Dr. Jenkins was the New Mexico State Historian and Archivist.

**ORLANDO ROMERO** – Writer of articles, stories and poems about life in Northern New Mexico. Mr. Romero is currently the Librarian of the History Library in the Palace of the Governors.

**JIM SAGEL** – Bilingual writer in the fields of fiction, poetry and journalism. In 1981, he was the recipient of the international literary award Premio Casa de las Americas for his book *Tunomas Honey*.

**MARC SIMMONS** – Historian/Writer has written articles and books on the Indian and Hispanic heritages of New Mexico. In addition, he is the author of a weekly history column which appears in several area newspapers. Dr. Simmons is a recognized authority on the history of the Santa Fe Trail.